AF328391

MARLOW MOSS

This book is from a series about Modern Women Artists published by Eiderdown Books.

Other titles available from the same series:

To order books, please visit eiderdownbooks.com

MARLOW MOSS

Lucy Howarth

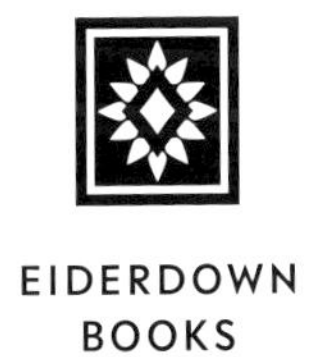

EIDERDOWN
BOOKS

MODERN WOMEN ARTISTS

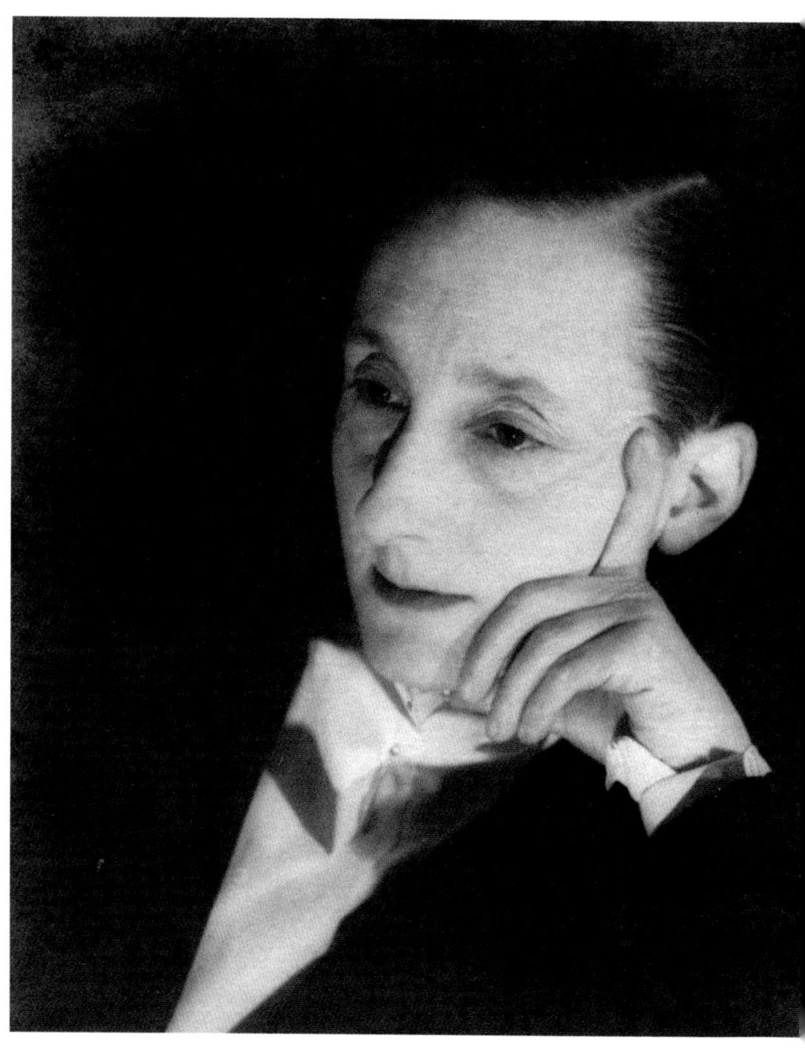

1. Stephen Storm, *Portrait photograph of Marlow Moss (leaning on her hand)*, c.1938

According to various accounts, Marlow Moss (1889–1958) was a biological realist, a recluse, a *persona non grata*, a phenomenon, a *Don Quixote,* a lone wolf and an Amazon. She was London-born and British, and, depending on perspective, she was also female, lesbian, and/or transgender (things get complicated); she was certainly an international Constructivist artist with a career spanning the 1920s to the 1950s. She was in the Paris circle of Piet Mondrian, and a student of Fernand Léger at the *Académie Moderne* in the late 1920s. She lived in continental Europe for many years, including France (in Paris and then Gauciel, Normandy) as well as the Netherlands. The Second World War had necessitated her repatriation to Britain, but she returned to Europe frequently after it was over.

Moss was a painter and a sculptor seeking to express 'space, movement, light', with drawing being central to her practice (Figs 19–22 and 26–7).[1] She was a contemporary, and friend, of European Constructivist artists such as Georges Vantongerloo, Jean Gorin and Max Bill. Moss was an atheist and an existentialist – yet she was also Jewish. This book aims to retrieve the artistic personality of Moss from this background, and illuminate her distinct contribution to modern art. As an artist, Moss cannot be located in one particular field of study, she instead traverses several: British art history, the history of Constructivism, feminist art history and gender studies (exemplified by her inclusion in this series) and queer theory (problematising, to a certain extent, her inclusion herewith). Moss disrupted and subverted her surrounding narratives; she was a British artist in Paris and a European in Cornwall; she was a female artist amongst men, but can be regarded as a pseudo-man amongst female artists. This resistance to categorisation is a large factor in Moss's obscurity; she is omitted from the histories because she does not fit in. To date she is most consistently discussed in reference to Mondrian, a paradigm that casts her in the role of follower, or worse, imitator. Moreover, despite living in Cornwall for nearly two decades, just a few miles from the celebrated St Ives Modernists, Ben Nicholson and Barbara Hepworth, there was barely any contact between them.

Miss/Moss

Wouter Stefan (Faan) Nijhoff – who worked under the name Stephen Storm – the son of Moss's Dutch life-long partner, Antoinette Hendrika (aka Netty) Nijhoff-Wind, made a striking series of queer photographic portraits of Moss (Fig. 1). In them Moss wears a cravat and jacket, like Mondrian's, her hair is short and brilliantined, her collar is high and her expression is composed – she makes a dashing protagonist.[2] Moss consciously and deliberately constructed an identity for herself. According to Netty Nijhoff's account, this was explicitly stated by Moss: 'I destroyed my old personality and created a new one.'[3] The origin of 'Marlow Moss' can be traced to a moment in 1919. Nijhoff is precise about the year Moss left the Slade School of Art in London, describing an emotional breakdown that was concurrent, and her transformation shortly afterwards. It is plausible, likely even, that Moss fell in love with a fellow student at the Slade, and that the 'shock of an emotional nature' referred to by Nijhoff, was heartbreak, possibly combined with the realisation of her sexual orientation.[4] However, the notion of a complete and self-conscious forging of a new personality in an instant, clearly owes something to Nijhoff's predilection for storytelling (she was a novelist after all), and a certain amount of self-mythologising from Moss herself.[5]

2

In the 1950s, Moss was mistaken for a man in several newspaper reviews, often resulting in a more favourable reception of her work. A *Sunday Times* reviewer claimed to have not known if Moss 'was a man, a woman, or a vegetable growth'.[6] Moss was assumed to be male, on account of her name and also based on the Constructivist art she produced, rather than her appearance. This is evident in memos from the director of the New York Museum of Modern Art in 1942, and anecdotally on numerous other occasions.[7] Despite these incidents of misconception, Moss's primary intention was for her new name to symbolise her post-gender identity, and perhaps provoke a double-take; 'Marlow' is an ambiguously gendered name, not a specifically masculine one.[8] Moss was not insistent on the use of her preferred name however: as late as 1932 she is listed as 'Marjorie Moss' in the first issue of the almanac *abstraction-création: art non-figuratif*, although she is simply 'Moss' after that, so perhaps she corrected them (Fig. 2). Signatures on earlier works tend to be 'M. Moss' until the 1940s, when she began to sign her works unequivocally 'Marlow Moss'. In letters to her friends however, and in all official correspondence, she always called herself 'Marlow Moss', from the earliest existent example of 1934.[9] In turn she was called 'Marlow', or 'Miss Moss', by everyone but her family.[10] Moss preferred not to have a gendering title preceding her name, as can be seen on her 1942 application form to the Artists' International Association, which she filled in very clearly 'Moss, Marlow (Marlow Moss)', but ignored the requirement to 'please state whether Mr, Mrs, or Miss'.[11] Whether or not Moss considered herself gendered, clearly others perceived her as such.

New Plastic

It is a gross over-simplification of Neo-Plasticism to attribute the development of this movement solely to Mondrian. Both Moss and Mondrian were Constructivists, which was Russian

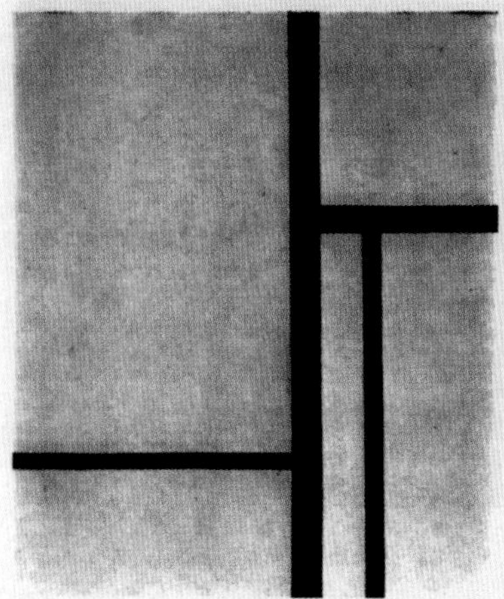

moss m . 1931 .

puisque c'est le but de cet almanach d'introduire le public dans le domaine de l'art non-figuratif, je veux me limiter ici a une brève explication des raisonnements qui m'ont poussée vers cette nouvelle plastique .

jusqu'aujourd'hui la peinture a employé comme moyen d'expression les formes déjà faites par la nature . pourtant le but de l'artiste n'a jamais été de donner simplement une représentation de ces formes . l'artiste se sentait attiré vers les formes naturelles , parce que malgré l'évidente muabilité de leurs formes limitées , elles semblaient lui communiquer une vérité immuable et universelle . sans éprouver pourtant le besoin d'approfondir cette vérité , il l'acceptait comme un mystère .

mais le peintre moderne ne se contente plus de ce sentiment de mystère . il suit ce raisonnement : si en effet les formes naturelles contiennent un élément d'une vérité universelle et immuable , cela veut dire alors que ces formes sont composées de deux éléments , c'est-à-dire d'un élément changeable en tant qu'elles sont formes visibles , et d'un élément inchangeable en tant qu'elles appartiennent à cette vérité universelle , et qui n'est pas visible . leur vraie valeur ne se trouve donc pas dans leur forme visible mais dans la relation qui existe entre cette forme et l'univers . la tâche de l'homme est donc d'approfondir sa conscience de l'univers afin de pouvoir établir l'équilibre de rapports qui doit exister mutuellement entre ces formes visibles et l'invisible . ayant formé une fois une conception mentale de l'univers il ne pourra plus se servir des formes naturelles pour exprimer cette conception . parce que ces formes naturelles et limitées , n'ayant qu'une valeur relative témoignent de cette vérité sans l'exprimer en sa totalité .

le peintre a donc été obligé de se créer une nouvelle plastique . voilà ce que l'art non-figuratif cherche à accomplir . il veut construire la plastique pure qui pourra exprimer en totalité la conscience de l'artiste envers l'univers .

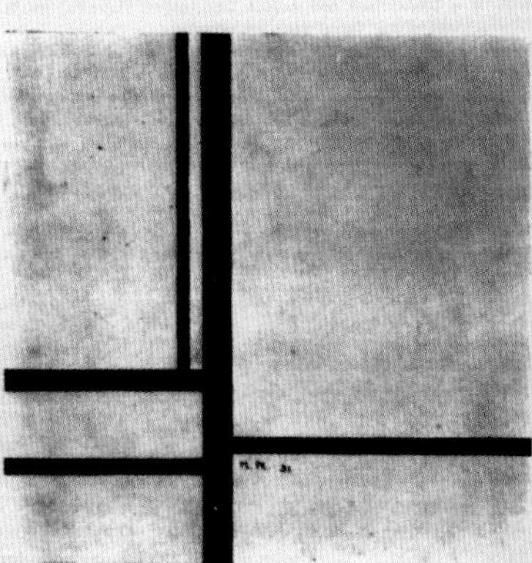

moss m . 1931 .

26

2. *abstraction-création: art non-figuratif*, Issue 1, 1932, Paris, p.26
(showing two paintings, both dated 1931)

originally, and then European; and there were many other significant artists involved in the movement too. In the Netherlands recently, great effort has been made, across many different events and exhibitions, to broaden our understanding of *De Stijl* (meaning 'The Style' in Dutch), thereby defusing the spotlight from Mondrian. *De Stijl*, with its underlying notion of the Neo-Plastic (or *Nieuwe Beelding* in Dutch, simply meaning 'new art'), was established in 1917 by Mondrian and Theo van Doesburg. Vantongerloo too was a key figure. Moss was not present for these early years in the Netherlands – at that time she was still struggling to discover her calling at the conservative art institutions of London: St John's Wood Art School and the Slade. She moved to Paris, by then the established centre of modern art, in 1927. There she joined in the formation of *Abstraction-Création* – an association of artists brought together in 1931 for the purposes of promotion and discussion of non-figurative art through exhibition and publication. *Abstraction-Création* was set up by members of *De Stijl* as well as others – Jean Arp and Auguste Herbin – and represented the unification of many factions of international non-figurative art. In other words it connected the émigrés with other groups of artists such as the Parisian *Cercle et Carré* and *Art Concret*. It ran until 1936, and published five annuals – Moss was the only woman and the only British artist to feature in all of them.

The achievement of *Abstraction-Création* was to establish a cohesive link between the varied and sometimes volatile membership of these groups of artists. Yet rows between artists such as van Doesburg and Mondrian still occurred, emanating from personality clashes, as well as serious artistic differences. Emblematic of their discord was a disagreement over the inclusion of the diagonal line in the grammar of Neo-Plasticism; Mondrian was for the vertical and the horizontal exclusively, whereas van Doesburg persistently introduced the dynamism of the diagonal (as did Moss, see Fig. 14 as well as most sculptures and drawings, and, depending on orientation, Figs 5 and 15). Whether or not Mondrian objected to the diagonal *per se*, or just any deviation from his own designs, is moot. Other tensions arose between van Doesburg and Vantongerloo, who fought at the preview of a 1930 *Cercle et Carré* show; while the relationship between Vantongerloo and Mondrian was also strained at times.

Abstraction-Création stood for rational and utopian non-figurative art, be it abstracted from nature, or constructed by mathematical calculation, as Moss's was (see Figs 26–7), contrary to the trend of romantic Surrealism. Moss intended '... to construct pure plastic art which will be able to express in totality the artist's consciousness of the universe.'[12] She entered the fray with her first Neo-Plasticist painting in 1929, and her first significant contribution to the development of the language – the double-line – came a year later. Two lines, running parallel: this innovation, and the disturbance it caused, announced Moss to the Neo-Plasticist avant-garde. Following on from this, in January 1931, Moss exhibited two paintings, both featuring a double-line, at the second '1940 Group' show with *Les Surindépendants* – another association of artists. These paintings were probably the two works that appeared in the first issue of the annual *abstraction-création: art non-figuratif*, published the following year (see Fig. 2). Moss had discovered that: '... the secret of form lies not in form itself but in the continual changing and shifting of forms ...'[13]

Double-Line

Mondrian, who knew Moss through Nijhoff, wrote to her asking what the purpose of the double-line was, and Moss responded with a lengthy explanation, including drawings and calculations. She explained that she found the single line grid, that Mondrian had been working with for over a decade, to be a 'conclusion and restriction' to a composition. Mondrian is

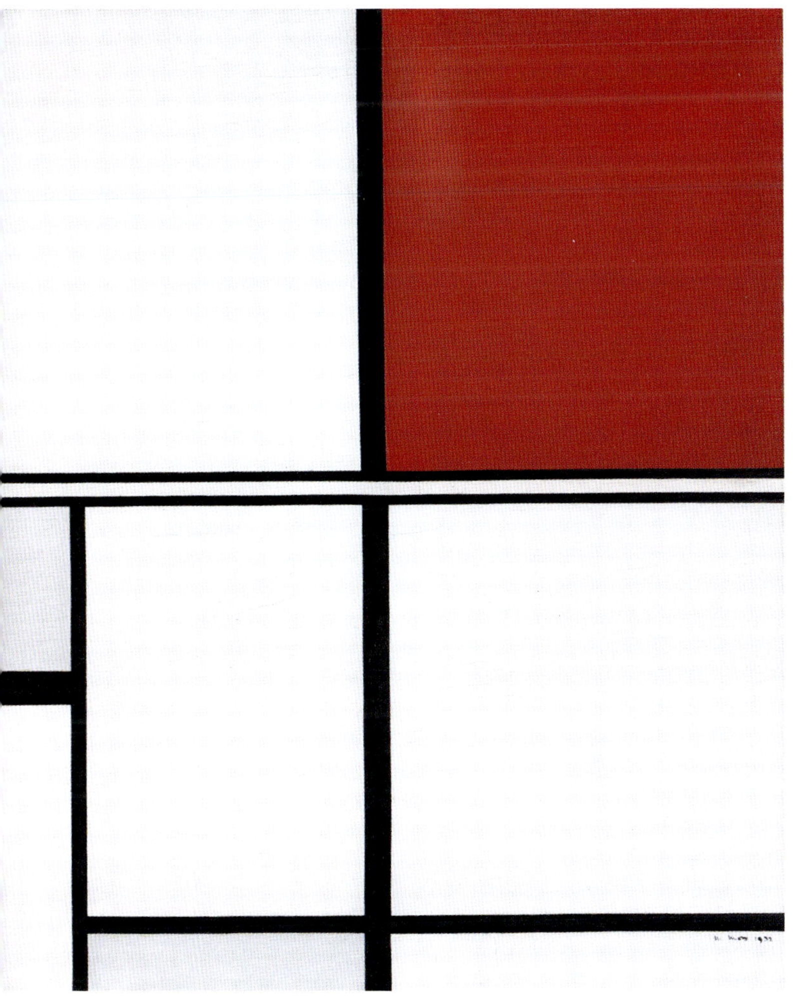

3. *White, Black, Red and Grey*, 1932, oil on canvas

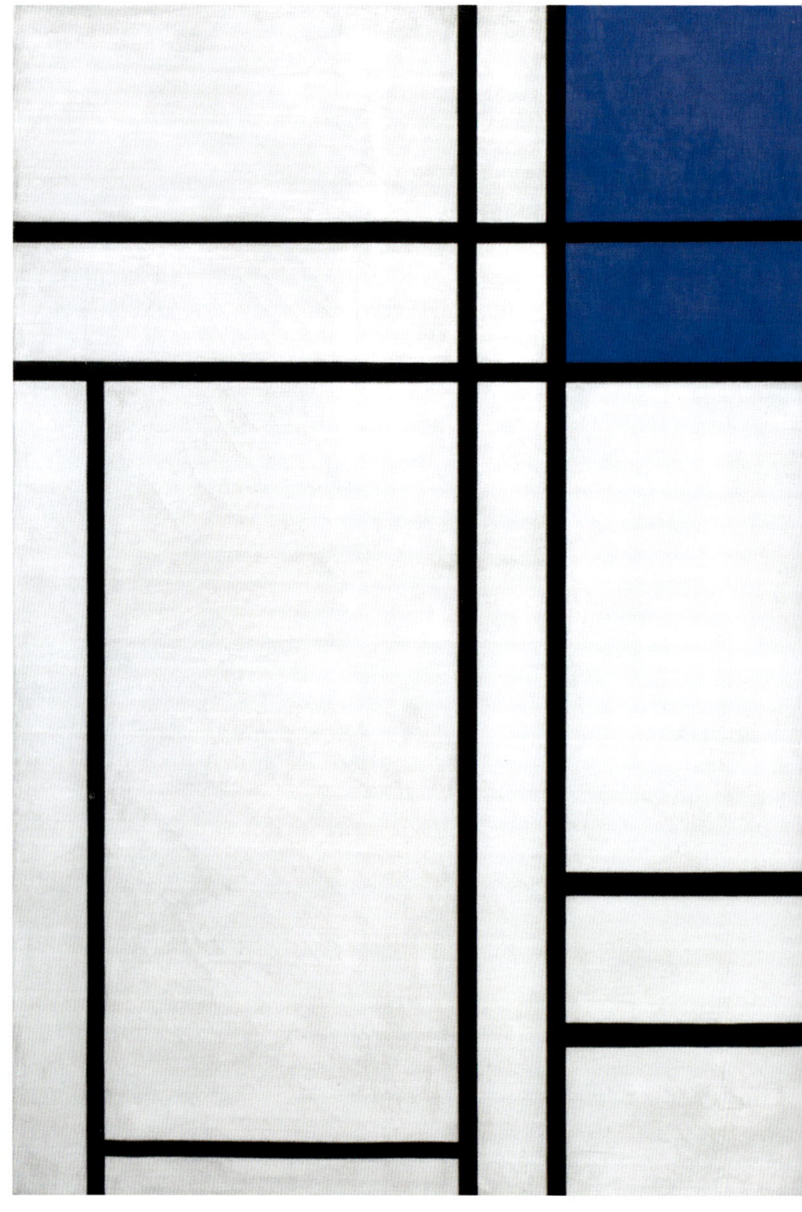

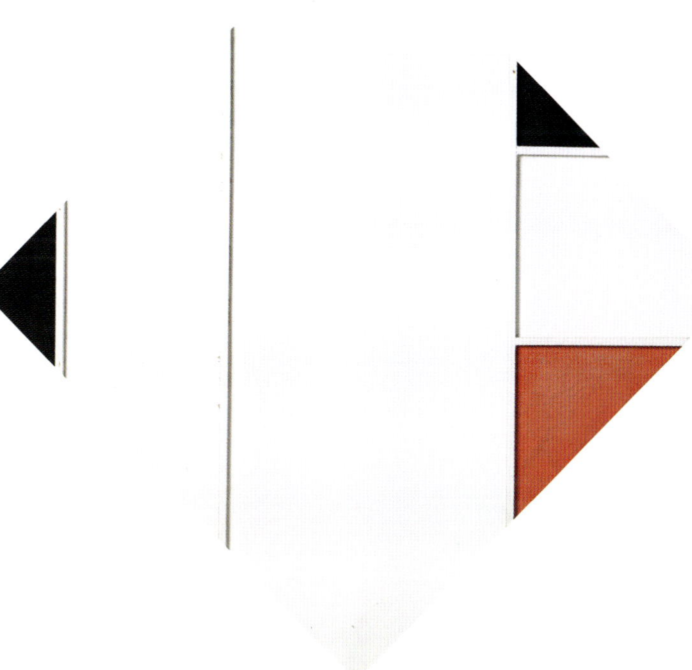

4. (opposite) *Composition With Blue Surface*, 1934, oil on canvas
5. (above) *White, Red and Black*, 1942, oil on canvas with wooden strips

understood to have responded: 'I couldn't quite follow your letter. Figures don't mean much to me'.[14] He subsequently wrote to Gorin asking his opinion on Moss's ideas.[15] The issue that most occupied Mondrian was the possibility that his Neo-Plastic language could be used to express a quite different personality, and the fact that Moss was a woman may have exacerbated his unease. Her use of mathematics and geometry (see Figs 26–7) was anathema to Mondrian. However, despite this, it was Mondrian who nominated Moss to Vantongerloo for membership of *Abstraction-Création.*

Moss and Mondrian became friends – inasmuch as Mondrian had friendships – and to a certain extent this can be traced through their letters to fellow artists. Mondrian expressed reservations about Moss as a Neo-Plasticist to Gorin in 1934: 'It seems to me that Miss Moss is at a less developed stage than you are, or at least at a less conscious stage . . .'[16] Tensions surfaced again, at least in Mondrian's mind, the following year, when he became offended at Moss's lack of attention to him during an illness. This perhaps indicates the gendered expectations he entertained, whether or not Moss was aware of them.[17] A warmer tone can be detected in Mondrian's telling of an incident when 'our little Moss' fell down stairs and broke a bone in her spine, which he reported with great concern.[18] Mondrian's later letters to Moss in the 1940s, if still formal (he always addressed her as 'Miss Moss'), reveal a distinct affection for her.[19] Nijhoff said of Moss: 'She understood Mondrian very well and vice versa. They were very well matched . . . a pair of extraordinary lone wolves.'[20]

Despite Mondrian's initial bewildered, or affronted, reaction to Moss's double-line (see Figs 2–4, 6 and 15), it subsequently formed a development in his own work, anticipating the syncopated jazz rhythms of his late New York paintings. Vantongerloo then accused Mondrian of stealing the double-line from Moss, adopting it without giving her credit.[21] It took several years for Moss and Mondrian to repair the damage to their friendship: probably as late as 1936 Mondrian remarked in a letter to Gorin that 'I am back to usual with her. It seems Vantongerloo had misinformed her about me – at least so much the better.'[22] Vantongerloo expressed resentment of Mondrian's monopolising of Neo-Plasticism in a letter to Gorin in 1937 in which he claimed that Mondrian enjoyed the veneration of Nicholson, Naum Gabo, László Moholy-Nagy and Henry Moore. Vantongerloo described these artists as the 'profiteers and parasites of abstract art', and allowed for a falsification of history, with regards to his solitary position, to take place as a result.[23] It is possible that such spats were the reason Gabo found Paris to be 'violent, gossipy and full of intrigue and jealousies'.[24]

Nevertheless, Moss and Mondrian rapidly developed the double-line theme, and both continued to include it, as a motif in various guises, for the rest of their respective careers; in the case of Moss the double-line appeared in her sculptural work too (see Figs 9 and 24–5). The originality debate, instigated in this case by Vantongerloo in defence of Moss, is conversely often used as an instrument to degrade the artistic standing of female artists; it is near-impossible to resolve. What can be a fruitful subject for analysis is the works themselves; in comparing the works of Moss and Mondrian from the early 1930s, a clear relationship can be seen. It is apparent that the two artists spent time together, and looked closely at each other's paintings. A mutual cause can be inferred, and a commonality of thought too; that was the ultimate goal of Neo-Plasticism afterall – to create a universal language of colour and form. The 1932 painting *White, Black, Red and Grey* by Moss (Fig. 3) is startlingly similar to Mondrian's *Composition B, with Double-line and Yellow and Grey* of the same year. These works are almost mirror images, and represent the moment when Moss and Mondrian were at their closest, artistically. It could be imagined that they painted them together, side-by-side – although actually their studios were a short

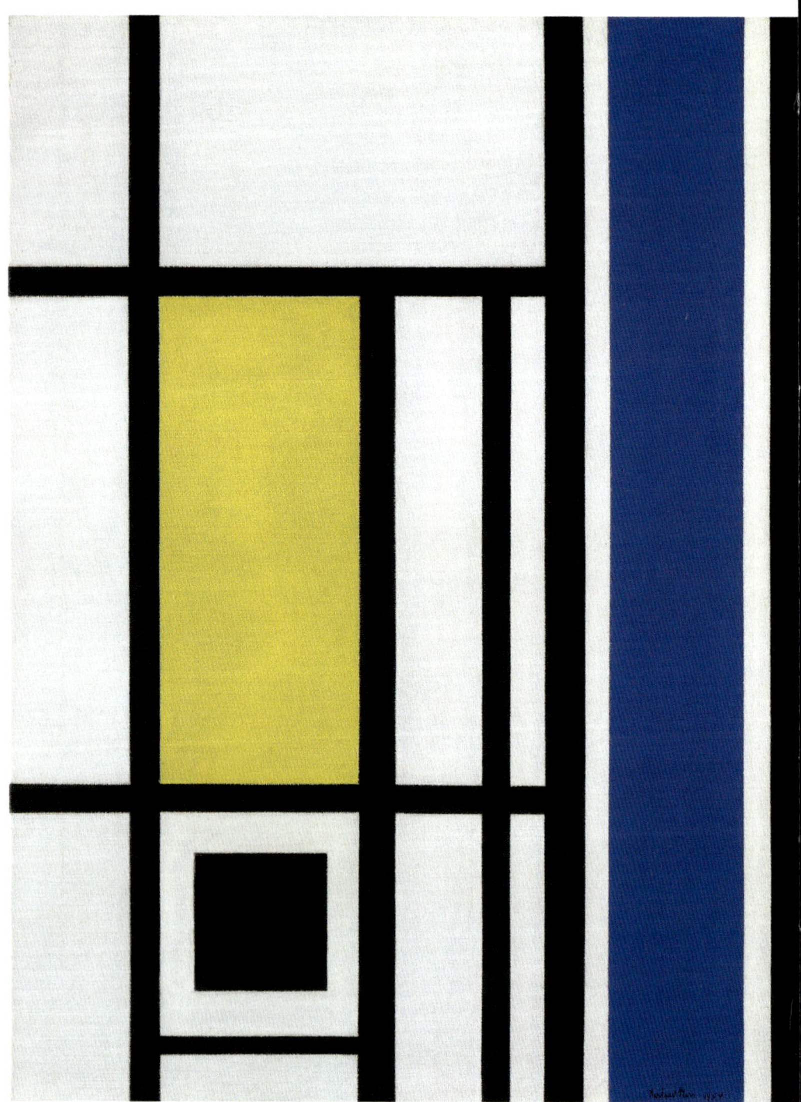

6. *White, Black, Yellow and Blue*, 1954, oil on canvas

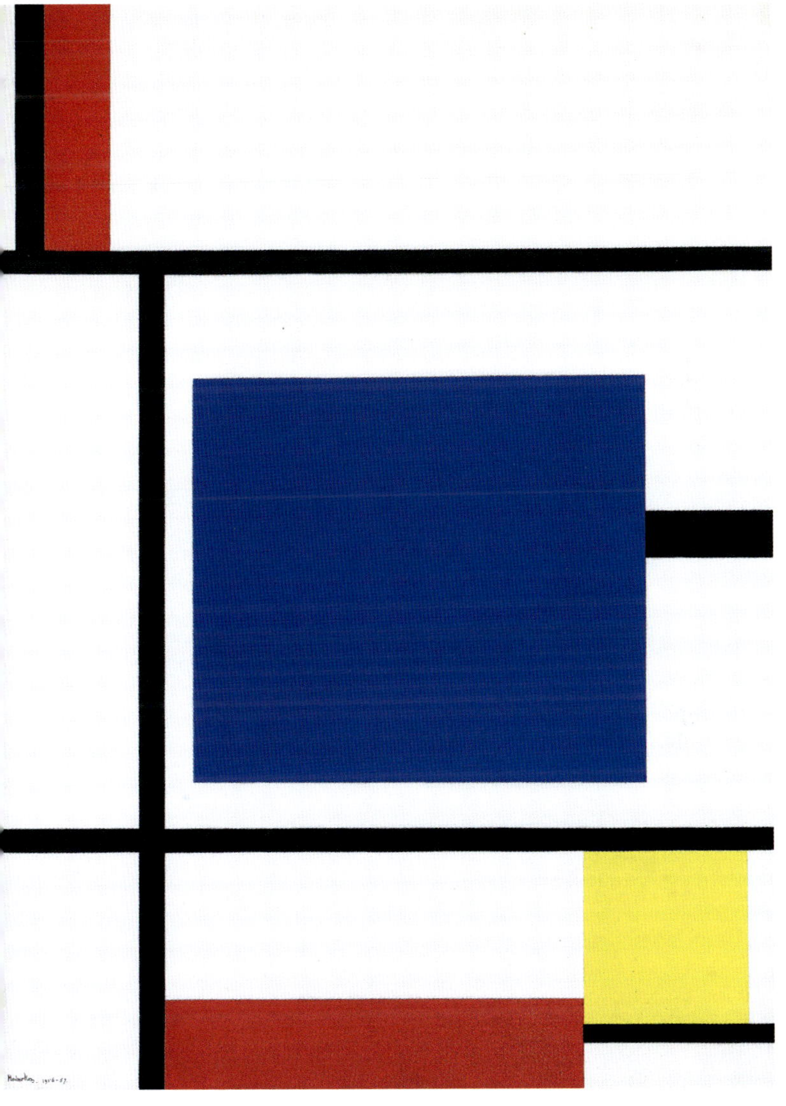

7. *Composition in Blue, Black, Yellow, Red and White, 1956–7*, oil on canvas

walk from each other, across Montparnasse. There is however, a crucial difference between the two paintings, other than the choice of red or yellow: Mondrian's double-line is bisected by a dominant vertical line; this has the effect of visually pinning it down. Consequently Mondrian's double-line remains, in fact, a line; that is to say the two lines form one single line. Moss's double-line, uninterrupted by the vertical, splits along its length; the two lines pertain to their corresponding areas, the upper and the lower, not just to each other. The narrow strip of white space allowed between the lines becomes incredibly activated, and, like the force between two repellent magnetic surfaces, the composition explodes outwards, and 'projects itself in all directions beyond the canvas'.[25] A continuous energy is generated – a *perpetuum mobile* – in sharp contrast to Mondrian's locked-down composition. In one of the few moments in Mondrian scholarship that the presence of Moss is dwelt upon, Cor Blok described the paintings thus: '[In the Moss] ... the upper and lower halves are forced apart by a movement that seems to go beyond the painting and con-nects it with its surroundings – which was also the artist's intention. Mondrian's composition remains within its frame; the two horizontals function as each other's echo.'[26]

This distinction clearly aligns Moss with Léger rather than Mondrian, despite surface appearances; the language Blok used is highly comparable to the way Léger's works are described to 'radiate energy about them'.[27] In contrast, Mon-drian's work, even when employing the double-line, is static and contained. Nijhoff described the reasoning Moss gave to Mondrian regarding the double-line: 'First: single lines split up the canvas so that the composition falls apart into separ-ate planes and the painting becomes a self-contained unit. Second: single lines make the composition static. Third: the double-line or a multiplicity of lines renders "a continuity of related and inter-related rhythm in space" possible, which makes the composition dynamic instead of static.'[28]

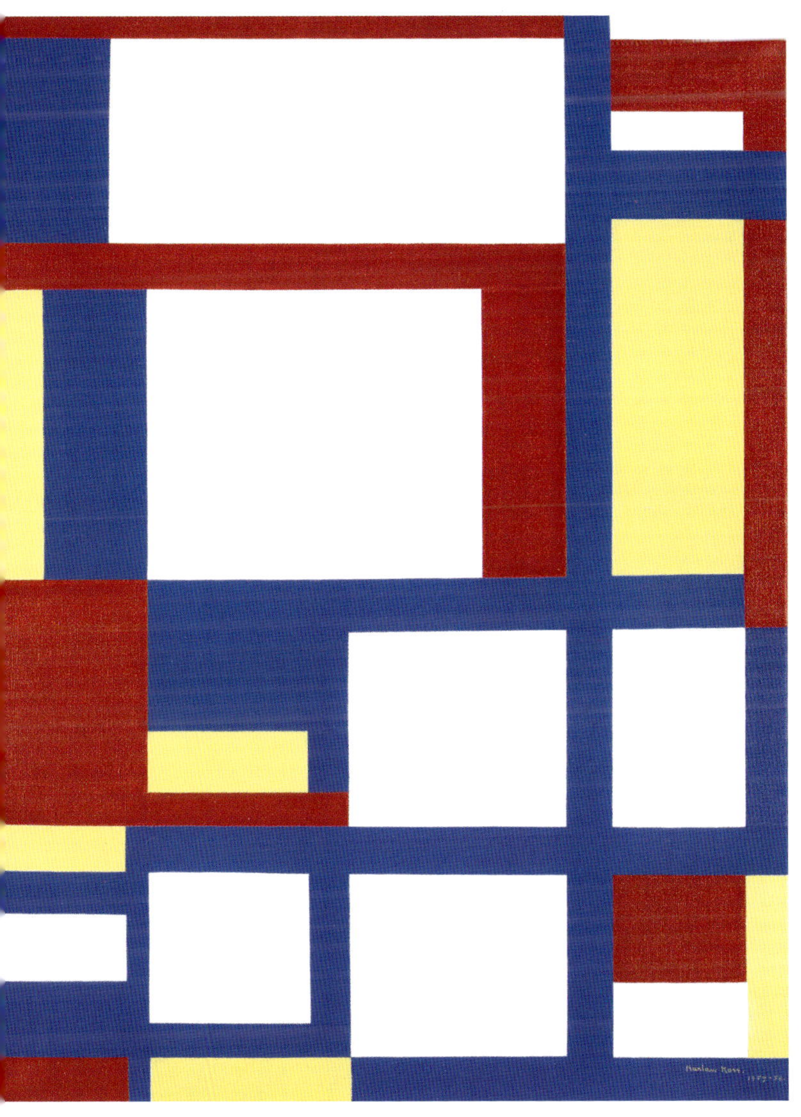

8. *Red, Blue, Yellow and White*, 1957–8, oil on canvas

Despite her life-long allegiance to Mondrian, Moss was not bound by his vision, as has often been assumed. From the beginning, she sought to develop an independent Neo-Plasticism of her own. This is not, however, how she has been represented; her usual epitaph is 'Mondrian's disciple'.[29] When she is mentioned in the *de rigueur* discussion of the double-line, it is emphasised that although it is possible that Mondrian had been 'inspired' by Moss to make this compositional innovation, his double-line is entirely distinct from hers.[30] In a vigorous re-framing of the facts, as set out by Nijhoff and Vantongerloo, in 1994 art historian Yves-Alain Bois wrote: 'Mondrian does not first criticize, and then adopt, Moss's invention, as Vantongerloo suggests; he is at first a sceptic, then understands his lack of interest in Moss's version, then demonstrates how, and for what destructive end, the double-line could be used in neo-plastic art.'[31]

There are a few references to Moss in Carel Blotkamp's Mondrian monograph, also from 1994:

> The last of the disciples deserving of a mention here is the English painter Marlow Moss, who in 1930–31 became fascinated by Mondrian's work ... the fact that the artist in question was a woman must have been somewhat embarrassing for Mondrian. He had always held firm views on the place of women and female artists within the cosmic order of evolution, views that today would be seen as decidedly sexist. And yet, during the 1930s it was due in part to impulses emanating from the work of 'Miss Moss' that he was prompted to introduce into his paintings a number of major changes.[32]

Although this paragraph is fairly sympathetic in tone, a different flavour can be detected in the language used to describe Moss as the 'disciple', and Gorin as Mondrian's 'colleague', juxtaposed upon the same page. Blotkamp argues in a similar vein to Bois, that it was Mondrian who devised the double-line in its most 'successful' incarnation – parallel lines of equal width and length – and in turn influenced Moss.

There are only two black and white thumbnail images of Moss works, both from *abstraction-création: art non-figuratif* (issues 1 and 3 respectively) (see Fig. 2), to serve as comparison with the large colour plates by Mondrian. When Moss is mentioned again in the text, during a discussion of Mondrian's vertically elongated canvases which 'may again have been borrowed from Marlow Moss', there is no illustration; rather an assertion that Moss's compositions are less 'radical'.[33] Moss is, however, credited with the introduction of coloured lines to Neo-Plasticism, along with several others (see Figs 8 and 19).[34] It is worth noting here that if the double-line has always been important in the reception of Moss, more recently it has been employed in the effort to adopt her into a canon of the queer.[35] 'Double' in this context evokes the Derridian double reading – and *différance* – or the Native American concept of a 'two-spirit'.

The lack of record of Moss's lost early works is problematic; she appears now only as a fully-fledged Constructivist, without a journey-to-abstraction back-story to humanise or legitimise her oeuvre. This trope of Modernism, exemplified particularly by accounts of Mondrian's work, pervades the apologia for abstraction; if there is no evidence that Moss could draw proficiently in an academic style, and no examples of early explorations via Impressionism for example, thereby demonstrating a personal artistic evolution, then there is an unease in accepting her as anything approaching a peer to the masters. When Moss is represented only by her later work, she is de-contextualised, and can more easily be dismissed as anachronistic.[36] Recent exhibitions that necessarily concentrate on the available later works have the same effect. If histories of art are customarily recounted as a series of revolutionary developments, then Moss can appear as a throwback. This is erroneous, yet while Moss's practice is historically located within pre-war European Constructivism, it is interesting to make connections between her work and other post-war movements

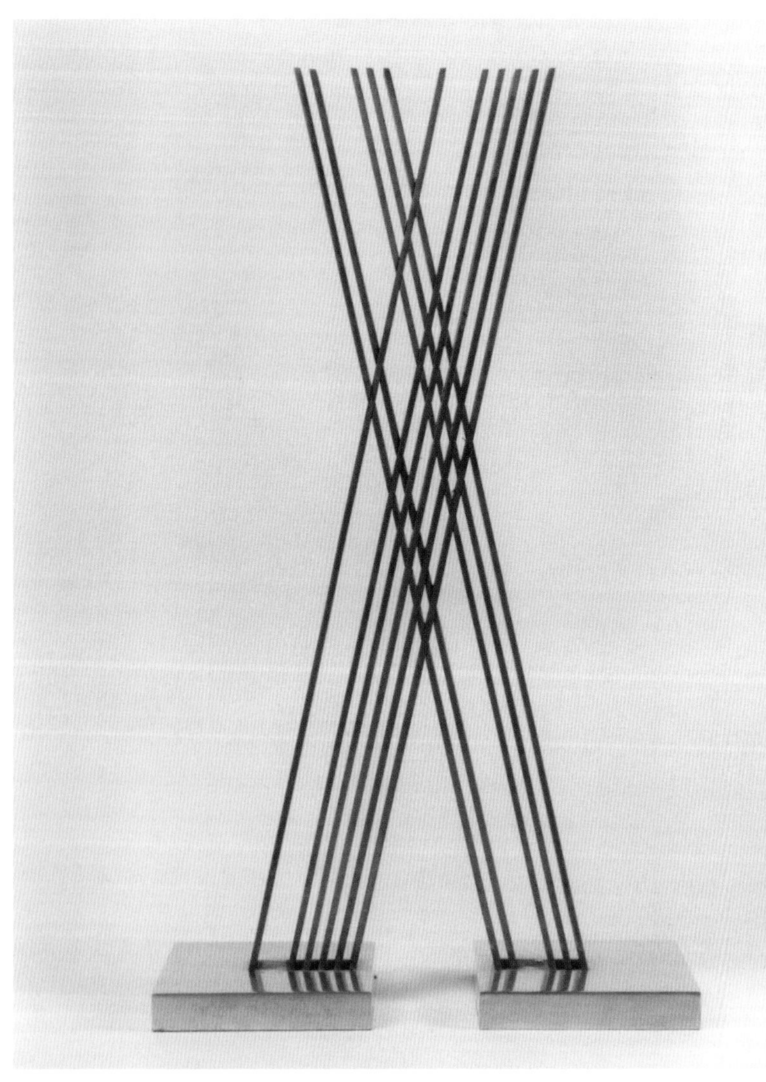

9. *Linear Construction*, 1956–7, steel, with aluminium bases

such as Conceptualism and Minimalism, and there is certainly an argument for a 'constructive tradition' of which she is part.

Eternal Return

Upon arrival in Cornwall in 1940 – marking her swift move out of Europe as a Jewish cross-dressing lesbian avant-garde artist – Moss took Mondrian's advice and wrote to Nicholson, who was the central figure of the St Ives School group of artists.[37] She asked if he and his wife (Hepworth) would like to visit her in Lamorna (just 12 miles away on the opposite coast), to discuss their work, with a view to putting on an exhibition. She was also seeking advice on whom to approach in order to show in London. As they had all been members of *Abstraction-Création*, and Mondrian was their mutual friend, Moss assumed that Nicholson and Hepworth would welcome her arrival in Cornwall. It is interesting that she did not write directly to Hepworth, invoking sisterhood of some-sort, especially as they had previously met in Paris; this may have been advised, but is most likely to have simply been in accordance with social convention of the time and seems like a missed opportunity as their sculptural sensibilities were more aligned. When Nicholson did not respond, Moss wrote again a year later. By her third letter, this time addressed to both Mr and Mrs Nicholson, another year later, it is evident that Nicholson had made a cursory reply.[38] Moss resorted to asking to borrow a copy of *Circle*, Nicholson's important 1937 publication, in the hope that this would give her some insight into the British art world.[39]

Although Moss and Nicholson did eventually cross paths, they did not become friendly or organise a show together in England in the manner that Moss had hoped. Various rumours circulated regarding the isolation of Moss from the St Ives artists, despite living close by for the remainder of her life. There are claims that Nicholson did invite Moss to exhibit in St Ives,

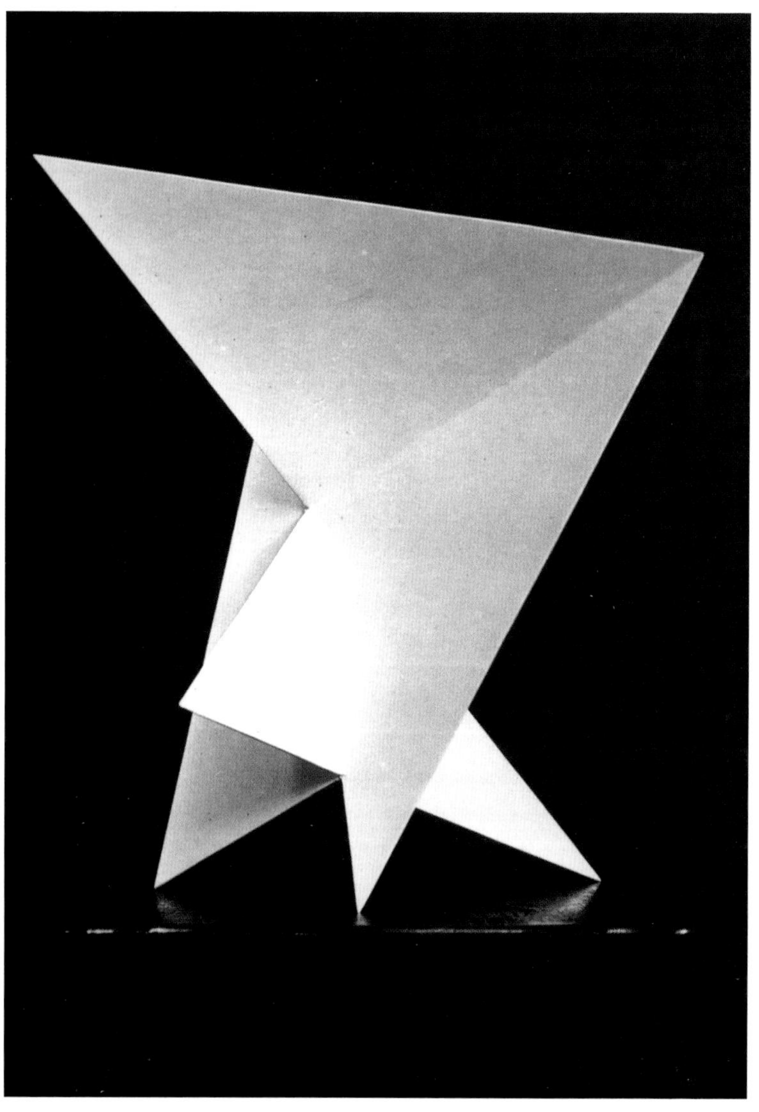

10. *[Triangles on Points]*, 1942–3, painted metal

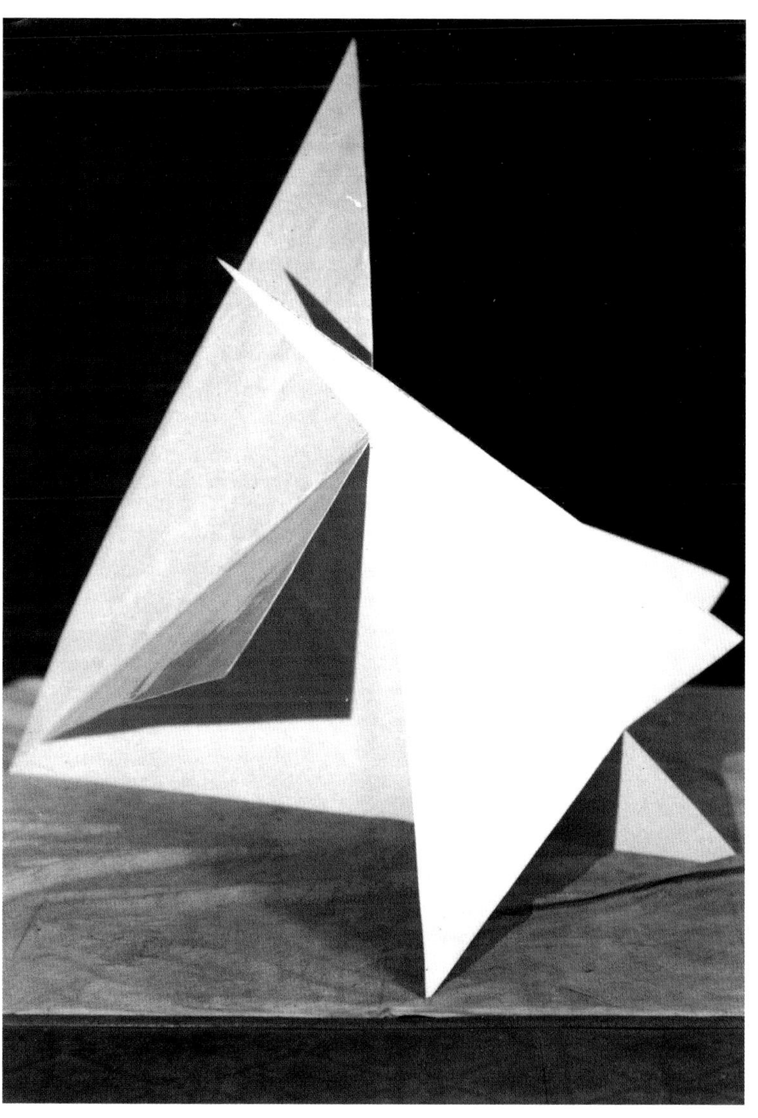

11. *[Triangles on edges]*, 1942–3, painted metal

and join the Penwith Society, but that she refused. Likewise, there are others who suggested that Moss at some point accused Nicholson of copying her work (they both made white painted wood reliefs), and therefore became *persona non grata*.[40] It is also alleged that Nicholson called Moss 'impure'.[41] This may have been in reference to Moss's departure from the 'rules' of Mondrian – her inclusion of diagonal lines and collaged material, and her use of curved lines and sculpture – however Nicholson himself never conformed absolutely to Mondrian's grammar. It seems therefore, if indeed he used the term, that Nicholson was referring to Moss's sexuality and gender identity. Either way there is something moralising about the choice of the word, especially as the notion of purity holds such significance for Constructivism. Although much of this narrative is fraught with supposition and tittle-tattle to say the least, overwhelmingly it does seem that Nicholson and Hepworth did not welcome Moss, and possibly deliberately used their influence to exclude her from the British incarnation of the Constructivist art movement. Moss commented in a letter of 1944 to Vantongerloo: 'I am very much alone in my ideas here. I have seen Ben Nicholson just once, things aren't going well between us, I don't even know why, so I never see him.'[42]

Moss made other local friends; her initial contact in Lamorna was Mrs Dodd, an old friend from the Slade (one can't help but wonder), from whom she rented a bungalow, and then the Impressionist painter Stanley Gardiner whom she would entertain, with his family.[43] Another friend was Susie Mitchell who apparently cleaned for Moss, and also accompanied her on trips abroad after the war.[44] Mitchell was eventually one of the beneficiaries of Moss's will, but it cannot be known if their relationship was simply professional, or friendly, or even romantic. Moss also knew artists in neighbouring Mousehole – the Surrealist painter Ithell Colquhoun, and Ruth Adams (also a painter, but all-but unknown) who is mentioned in a letter from Moss to Gabo, arranging a visit from the two of them.[45] It is likely that Moss knew Gluck, a more celebrated artist, and another sporadic resident of Lamorna, who took over her bungalow as a studio after Moss's death in 1958. Gluck underwent a transformation similar to Moss's, wearing groomed short hair and tailored suits.

Love and War

Moss had kept a separate studio in the village – a carpentry workshop that she renovated into a clean white space, flooded with light from the south (Figs 12–13), much like her pre-war studio in her home the Château d'Evreux in the village of Gauciel. Alongside a study of architecture, she made sculptures, enlisting a local shipyard in their fabrication. Moss also continued with the white reliefs using wood and cord that she had begun to experiment with before the war in Walcheren, when she had found herself stranded at the Nijhoff family home in the southern Netherlands (the Château was requisitioned by the French military). It is likely that, as she had found on Walcheren, it was impossible to obtain the canvases, paints and brushes that had been available to her in Paris; her move into sculpture and monochrome relief may have been pragmatic (Figs 9–11, 14–15, 17, 23–5, 28 and 31). She returned to painting in colour without relief elements eventually, but continued her experiments with sculpture until the end of her life.

During the war, in 1942, Moss exhibited at the American–British Art Centre in New York – perhaps thanks to Mondrian, with whom she remained in contact. Moss and Vantongerloo also stayed in touch throughout the war. In 1944 she wrote to tell him that Mondrian had died in New York, and that she had heard from their mutual friend the young Swiss artist Max Bill. Moss wrote about her work, and enquired about his:

Needless to say I'm very curious to see what you have done between 1940–1944. Bill wrote that you have worked a lot despite

all the difficulties. I am also pursuing my ideas, what I am doing
at the moment is very different from what you saw the last time
you came to Gauciel, i.e. the constructions in space.[46]

The six-year period of the war was a time of isolation and
uncertainty for Moss. A good deal of her money was tied up
in the Château d'Evreux, and was, along with her possessions
and work, inaccessible (it was all destroyed by a bomb in
1944 and she waited many years for compensation). The British avant-garde such as it was, had rejected and ostracised
her. She had few opportunities to exhibit her work, or mix with
contemporaries. The professional associations she was accus-
tomed to in Paris took the form of loose social affiliations
in England, and membership was not open to her. Once the
war was over, Nijhoff was able to join her in Lamorna, and
Moss began to exhibit in Paris once more, with the *Salon des
Réalités Nouvelles* at the Galerie Charpentier in 1946 and 1950.
From this point onwards, Moss and Nijhoff divided their time
between Lamorna, Paris, Walcheren and a houseboat on the
canals of The Hague. Together they sought out a European
community of lesbians and artists; traces remain of the
friendships they fostered with such people as the writer Anna
Blaman and Marika de la Salle (Fig. 17).[47] At times Nijhoff left
Moss unaccompanied in Lamorna and seemingly she conduct-
ed a couple of other love affairs. In an extraordinary text by
Colquhoun, in which the tangles and intrigues of the residents
of Lamorna are recorded, we learn the following:

> Miss Moss and Mme Nyhof [*sic*] lived together. Miss Moss had long
> ago had a relationship with Miss Palmer, who lived with Mrs Dodd.
> Miss P had also had a relationship with Miss Gluck. Mme Nyhof
> went to Holland; Miss Moss had an affair with a mutual friend of
> theirs who lived in a caravan at Trecastle (Tintagel, Boscastle), a
> cripple. The cripple wanted this to be permanent but Moss turned
> her down. Moss suggested living with Janet but Janet turned her
> down. Mme Nyhof came back.[48]

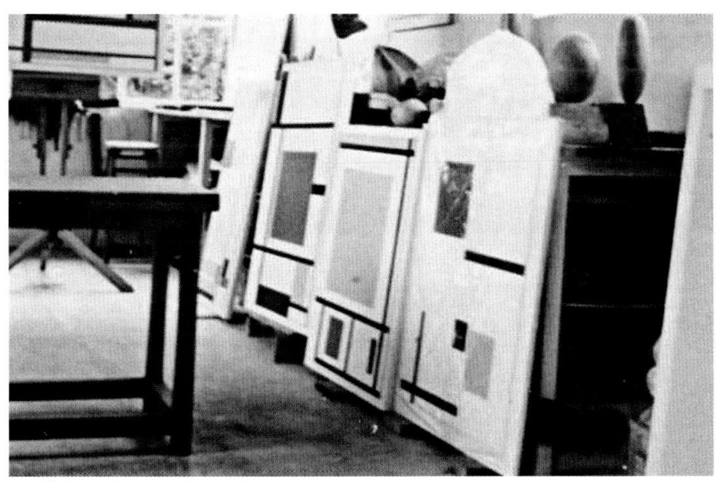

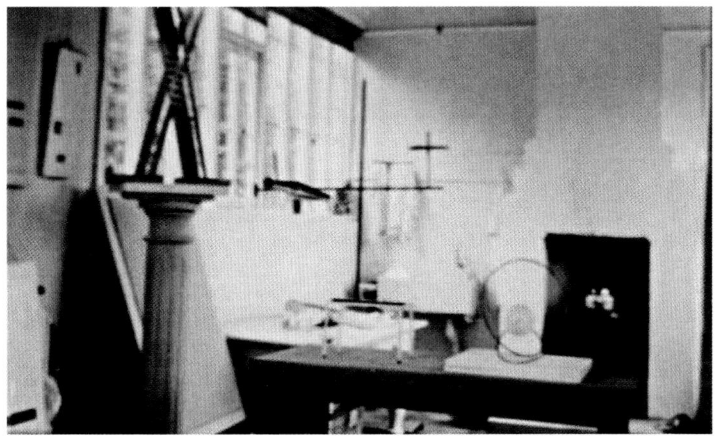

12. (above) and **13.** (below) Marlow Moss's studio in Lamorna, *c.*1956–8

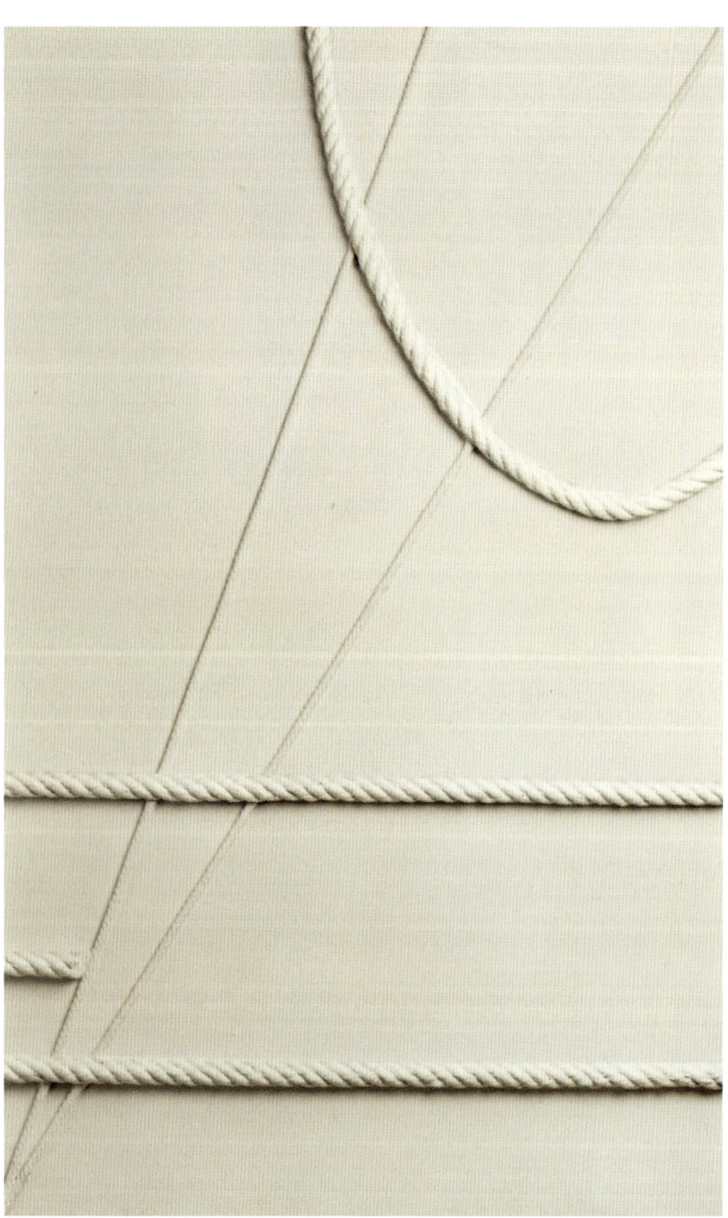

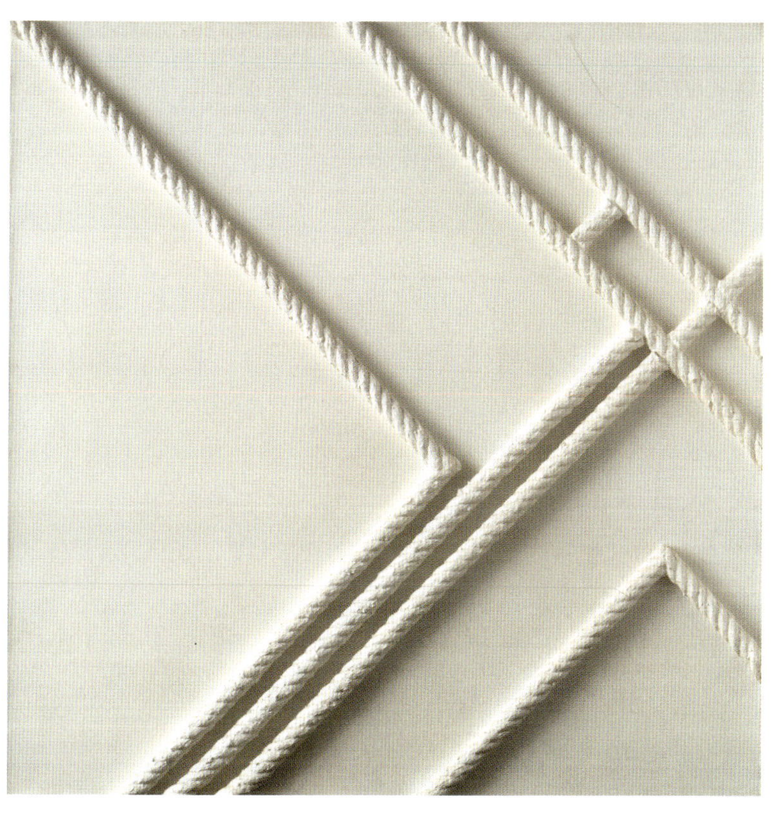

14. (opposite) *White with Curved Cord*, c.1936, oil on canvas with cord
15. (above) *White with Rope*, 1940, oil on canvas with rope

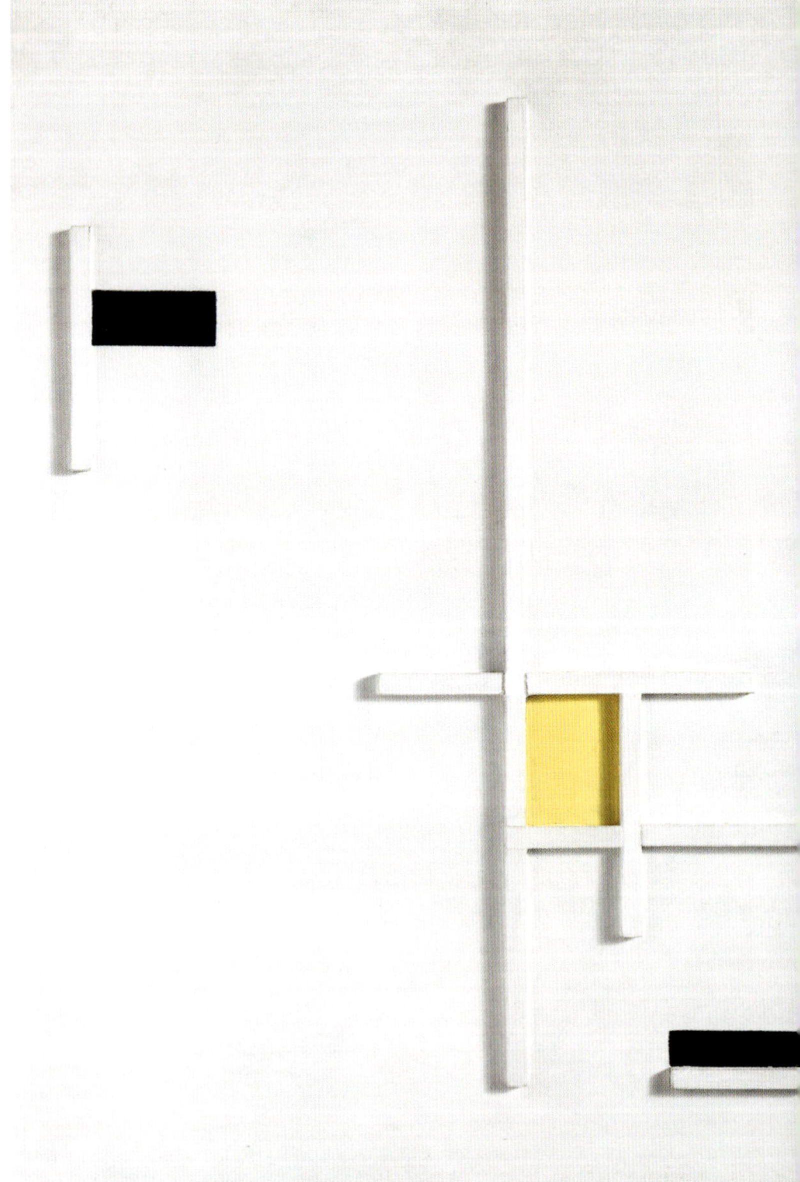

An affair with Ruth Adams also seems a possibility. Moss had at least two exhibitions locally at the Arra Gallery in Mousehole, belonging to Adams's married lover, the Austrian artist Albert Reuss (the name 'Arra' is their initials combined).[49] The text from one of the accompanying catalogues gives Moss's characteristically compact account of her work:

> I would like to ask the public to look at the work, as free as possible from preconceived ideas on art. These drawings are constructed on a very simple principle – a geometrical figure – sometimes broken, sometimes cut, sometimes divided, sometimes subdivided – until the relation of the lines to each other produce an aesthetic emotion.
>
> If one considers the lines in these drawings as sounds (note or chord progressions) and geometrical figure as the musical key, one can, to a certain extent, compare these drawings to music.
>
> Music is the 'art of combining sounds with a view to beauty of form'; this work aims at 'beauty of form' by coordinating form and line on the plane.
>
> Quoting from Plato . . . what I understand by beauty of form is, something characterized by straight lines and circles, surfaces, and solid bodies composed with the straight line and the circle by means of the compass, the set-square and the plumb. For these forms are not like the others (natural forms), beautiful under certain conditions, but they are always beautiful in themselves . . .[50]

Space Movement Light

Moss was given a solo show in 1953 at the Hanover Gallery in London, by the director Erica Brausen, and then again in 1958, just a few months before Moss's death. Brausen, 10 years younger than Moss, had moved to Paris from Germany in the 1930s. She was involved in the avant-garde scene, and it is likely that she knew Moss from there, either through artist friends

16. *Composition in Yellow, Black and White*, 1949, oil paint and wood on canvas

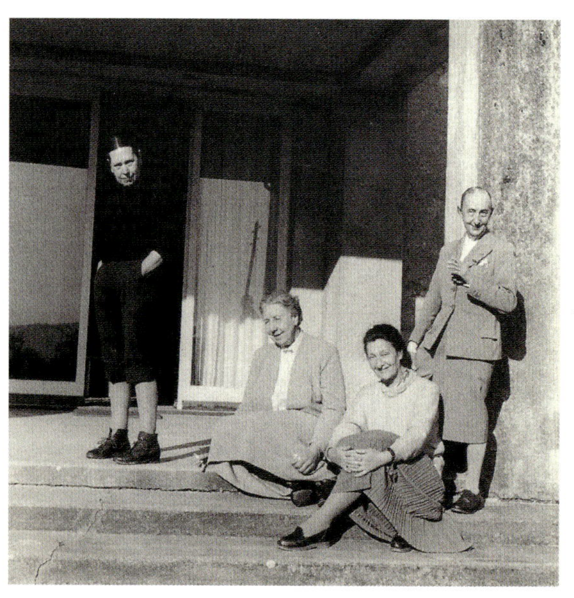

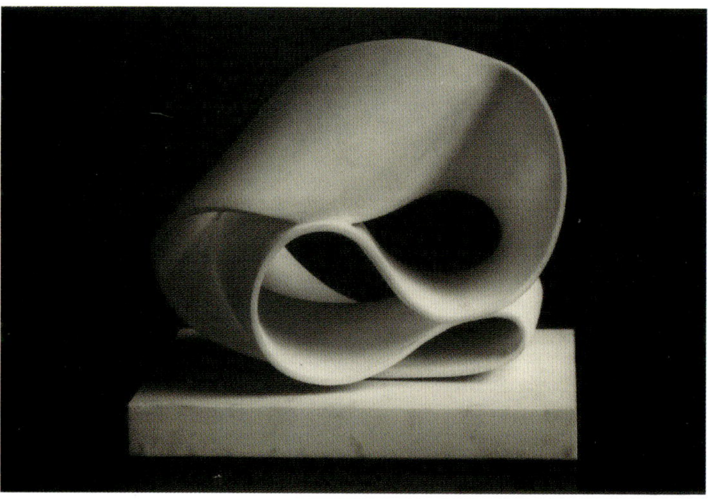

17. (above) Marika de la Salle, Netty Nijhoff, Ireen Farjon and Marlow Moss, *c.*1950s **18.** (below) *Sculptural Form*, 1943, white marble

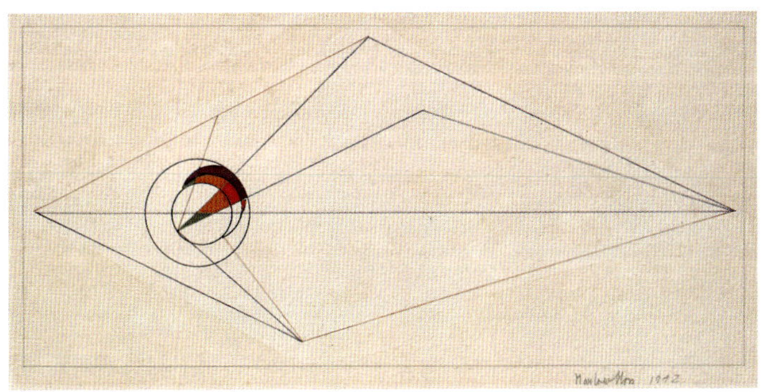

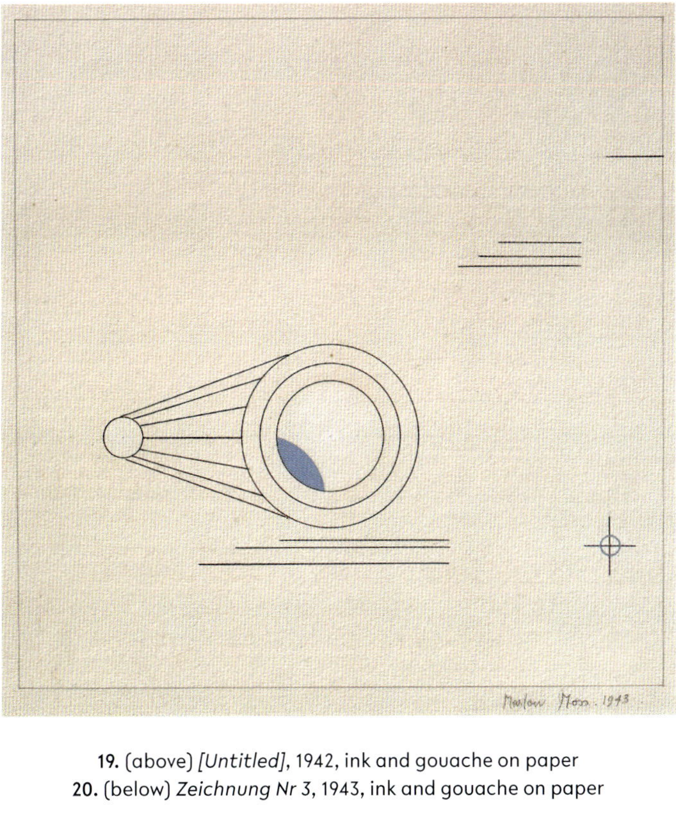

19. (above) *[Untitled]*, 1942, ink and gouache on paper
20. (below) *Zeichnung Nr 3*, 1943, ink and gouache on paper

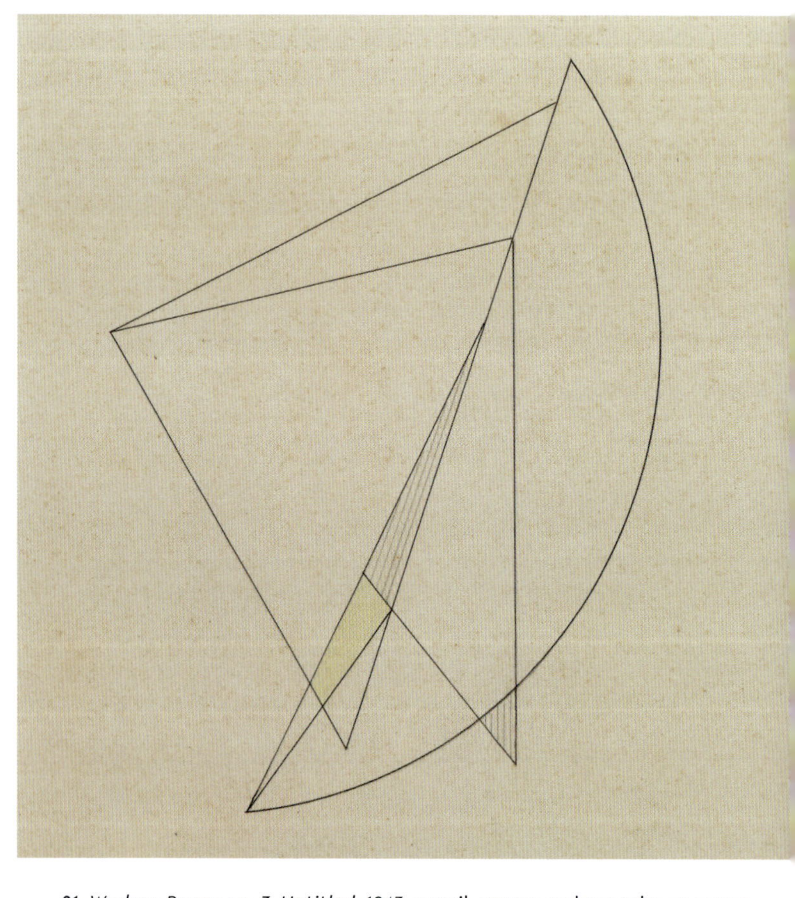

21. *Work on Paper, no. 3, Untitled*, 1943, pencil, crayon and gouache on paper

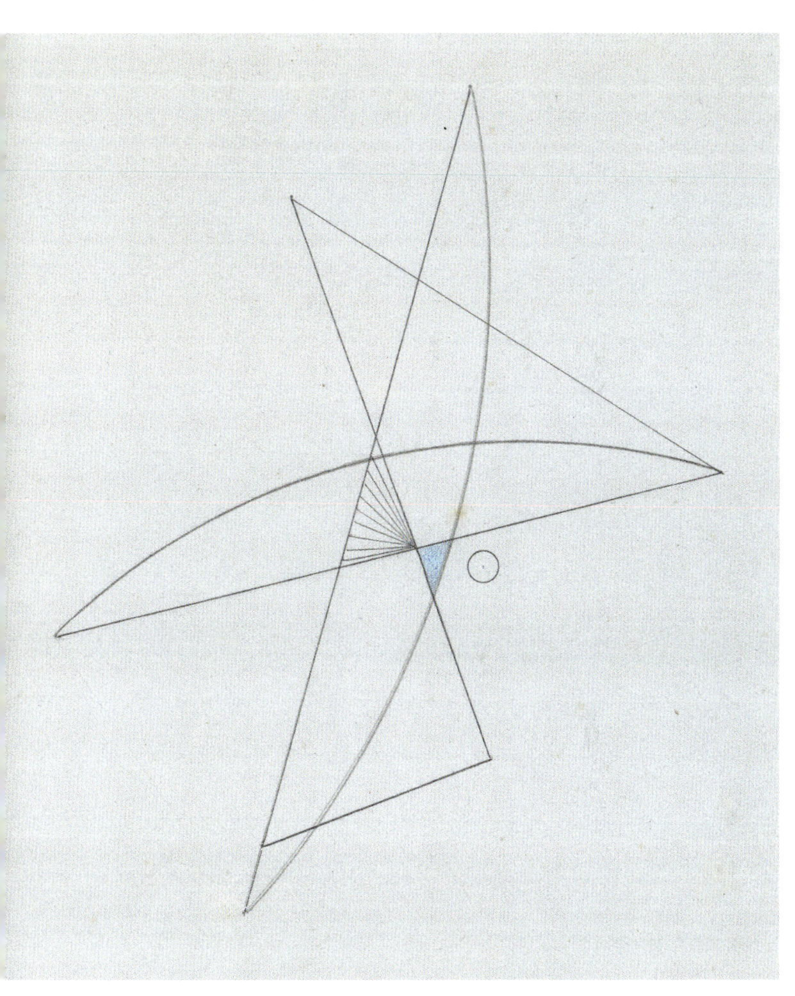

22. *Untitled*, 1946, pencil and crayon on paper

(she knew Mondrian), or through the gay café network: the two worlds intermingled. From Paris she went to Majorca, possibly with Joan Miró, where she ran a bohemian bar. She harboured Jews and socialists during the Spanish Civil War, providing an escape route stopover. Like Moss, Brausen arrived in London at the start of the Second World War. She married a homosexual friend to gain British citizenship, and worked at the Redfern Gallery on Cork Street. In 1947 she set up the Hanover Gallery in Mayfair.[51] She exhibited mainly European artists, with a Surrealist bent; but also some British – it is unclear why particularly she took on Moss.[52] Moss described Brausen as 'very moody and not easy' in a letter to the British artist Paule Vézelay, but added that she was always very friendly to Moss herself. Her assistant remembered Brausen as 'sharp and precise', which perhaps also characterises the qualities of Moss's work that appealed to her, or perhaps it was more personal.[53] Moss and Vézelay had a long friendship and successfully collaborated with the 1955 British *Groupe Espace* exhibition at the Royal Festival Hall on the South Bank.[54]

It must be emphasised that to present an ambiguous gender identity in the mid-twentieth century was no small act of bravery. It was against French law for a woman to dress in male clothing, and Moss and Nijhoff were on occasion cursed and spat at when they ventured outside of Paris.[55] The incident of their arrest in 1940, by Dutch authorities, on suspicion of being German soldiers disguised as women, serves to demonstrate the dangers of causing 'gender trouble'.[56] If Moss's sartorial style read as male, that may have also been conflated with her being anti-female – a charge compounded by the reading of Moss's work itself as a denial of her sex, assuming of course that her aesthetic of hard straight lines denotes masculinity.[57] The existence of Moss, a woman and a Constructivist, challenges the notion of 'hard' geometric art as necessarily masculine, and presents a challenge to gender essentialism, be it feminist, trans or misogynist. Moss's gender identity and sexual orientation could be construed as barriers for a feminist account that demands a female subject, if a lesbian is not a wo-man or a fe-male (an appendage of a man). This discourse maybe goes some way to explain the lack of feminist scholarly interest in Moss – the one exception being Germaine Greer: 'A superficial judgment would place Marlow Moss as an imitator of Piet Mondrian . . . but in fact the relationship between them was one of equals, and in the case of the double-line composi-tions, Mondrian followed the lead set by Moss . . . It is arguable that she had a greater influence on subsequent developments in twentieth-century painting than Mondrian.'[58]

Without Prejudice

Moss has attracted unusual artistic reactions. *Marlow Moss Reconstructieproject*, by Florette Dijkstra, comprised of small-scale reproductions and images of Moss's known oeuvre in acrylic (Fig. 29). The accompanying publications are unconven-tional art history.[59] Together they are a double reading of Moss's work, and Moss herself. Alternative modes of engagement continue to arise; there has been an operetta and a choreo-graphed dance about Moss, and more recently an album of electronic music.[60] *For Marlow Moss* is an arcade canopy in glass and metal by Andrew Bick, installed above Princes Arcade on Piccadilly, London, as a permanent tribute to Moss (Fig. 30). Bick has also designed a Moss pocket square for Drake's Mens-wear – a particularly fitting tribute for such a natty dresser. Curators have staged exhibitions around Moss, and artists have made work referencing or celebrating her.[61] It has even been suggested, somewhat facetiously, by one British critic that Moss 'never existed at all' and is instead 'one of those fictional artists that artists invent'.[62] In an essay that examines such practices, and so-called 'whole history' projects, Rex Butler, discussing Moss through the prism of Dijkstra's work, posits that an exhibition of Moss's work can only be 'anti-climactic'

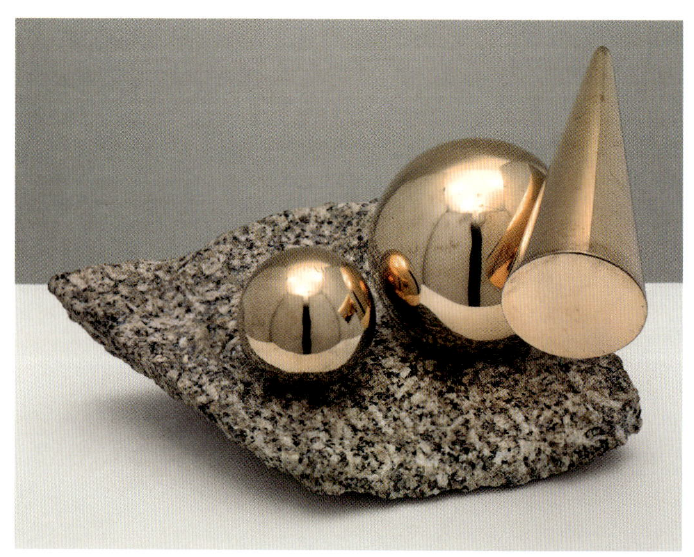

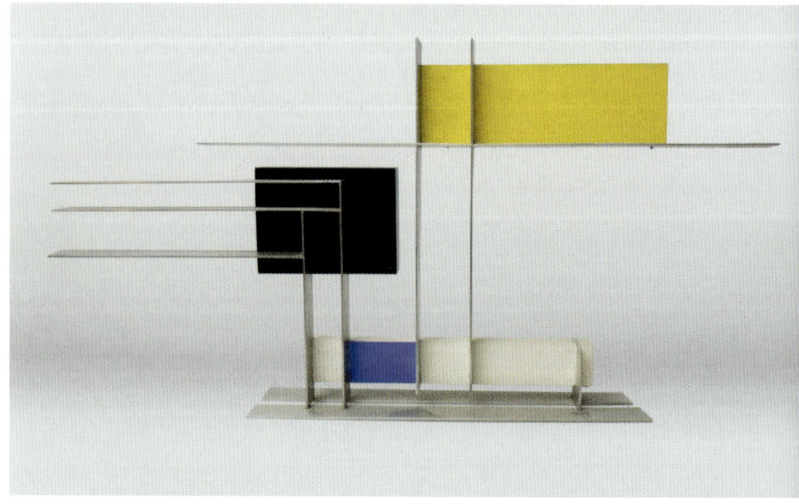

23. (above) *Balanced Forms in Gunmetal on Cornish Granite*, 1956–7, metal and granite 24. (below) *Free Relief*, 1957, painted wood and aluminium
25. (opposite) *Spatial Construction in Steel*, 1956–8, steel

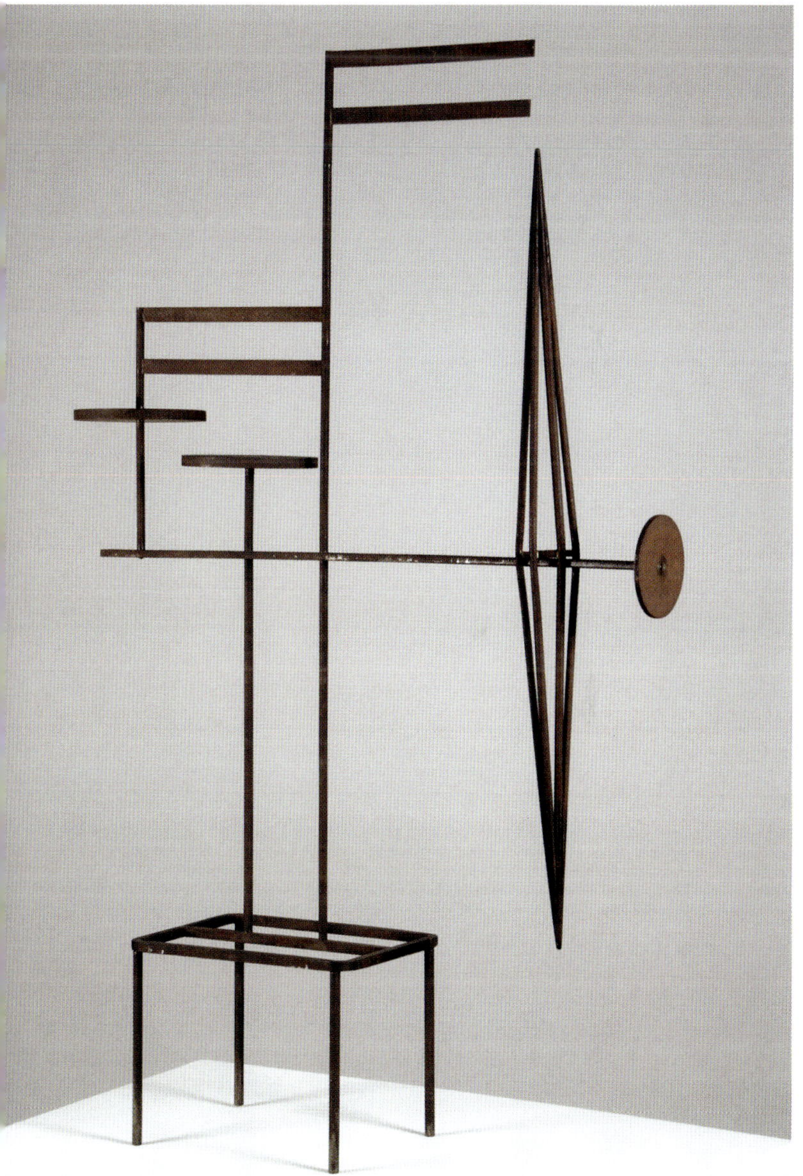

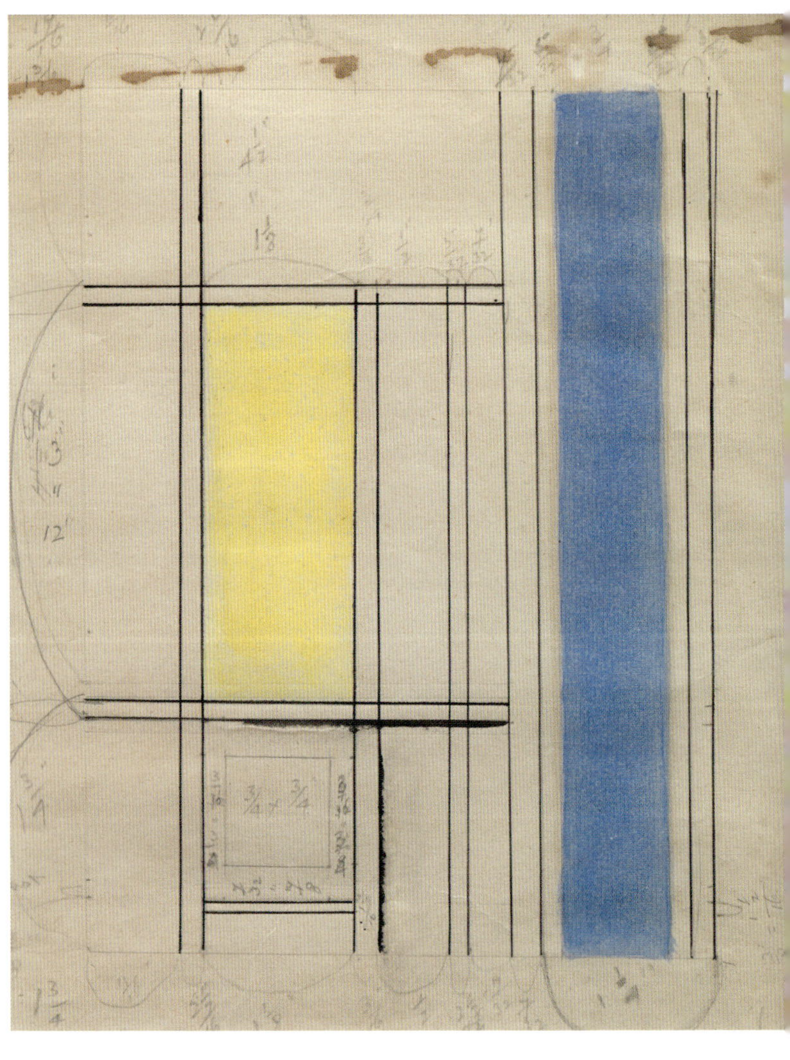

26. *No.31 preliminary drawing for oil, c.1954, pencil and gouache on paper*

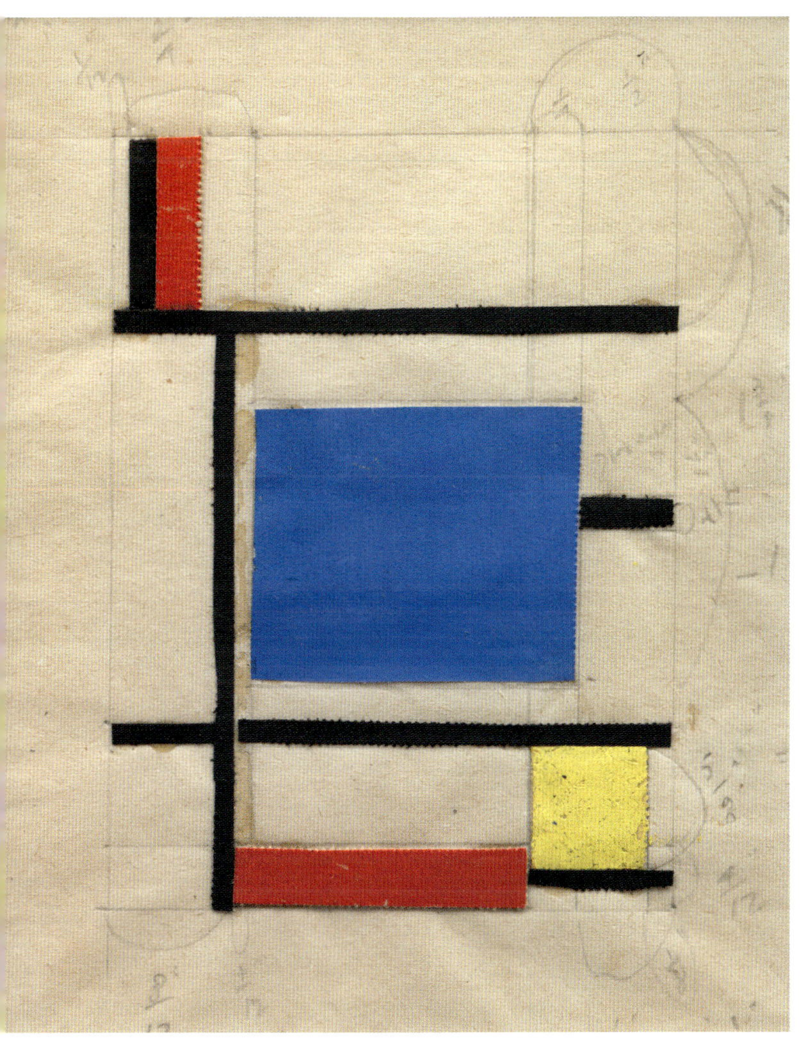

27. *No.34 preliminary drawing for oil, c.1956, pencil, collage and gouache on paper*

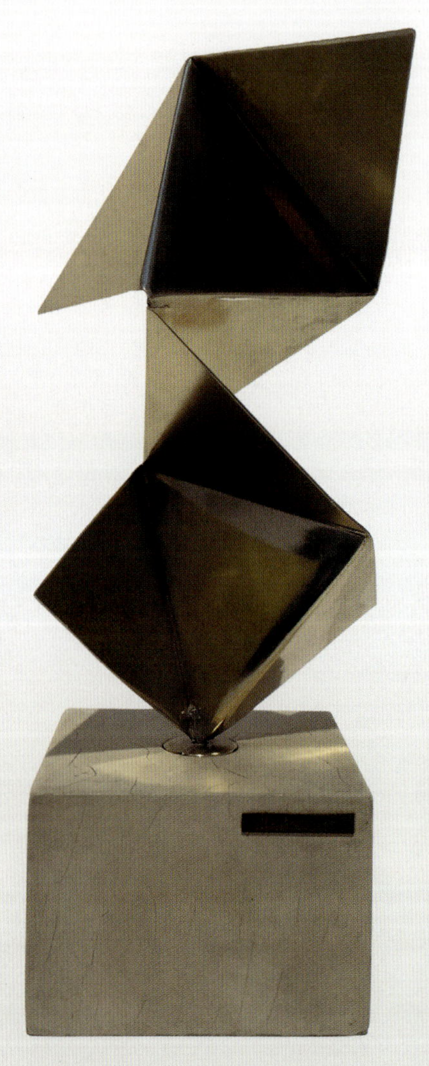

and 'merely a reversal of prior erasure'.[63] There is a danger that Moss's status as a forgotten woman could eclipse her achievements as an artist. Her unknownness itself has become an attribute; she serves as an example of the remissly neglected, useful to destabilise accounts of Constructivism.[64] This was not, however, her position during her lifetime, when she was acknowledged by her contemporaries as a comrade. Mondrian urged her to do as he had done and emigrate to New York where the modern movement was flourishing.[65] If she had gone, or if she had exhibited alongside Vantongerloo, as he proposed, in New York, Moss might now be more recognised in the history of new plastic art.[66]

It is arguable that Moss's critical reputation within accounts of the Constructivist movement has suffered from one key act of omission – her absence from the aforementioned 1937 publication *Circle*.[67] Moss was not in England during the period of this publication, but if she had been working in London at the time, rather than on the Continent, it would have been more difficult for the editors to ignore her.[68] If Moss had appeared in *Circle*, she may have subsequently featured in Charles Biederman's book *Art as the Evolution of Visual Knowledge* in 1948, and then in George Rickey's *Constructivism* and the anthology *DATA*, both published in the decade following her death.[69] Her absence from all of these accounts makes it almost inevitable that she does not feature in other surveys such as Stephen Bann's 1974 publication *The Tradition of Constructivism*.[70]

Becoming

Over the years, when I am asked who Marlow Moss is, I often resort to the familiar phrase 'the female British Mondrian', as this was how she was first described to me. It is, of course, a shorthand explanation, the truth being far more complicated.

28. *Untitled*, c.1950s, brass on wooden base

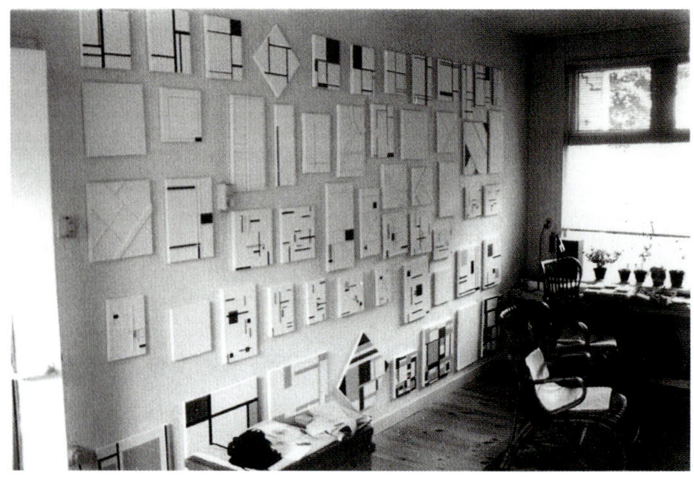

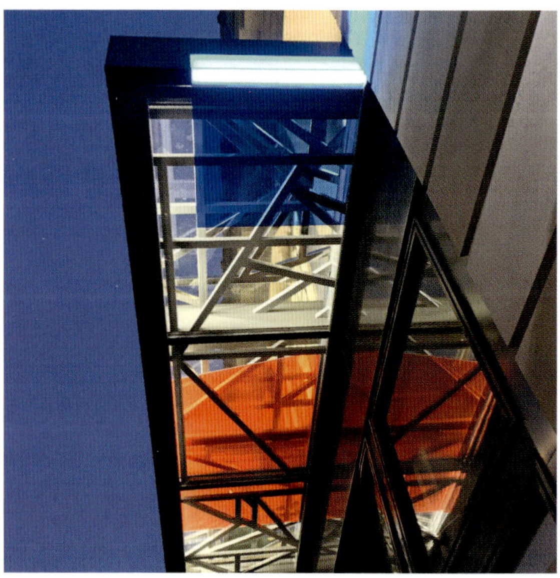

29. (above) Florette Dijkstra, *The Marlow Moss Reconstructionproject*, 1994
30. (below) Andrew Bick, *For Marlow Moss*, 2018, aluminium, bronze, glass and stainless steel

However, it is effective in communicating to people the sort of thing I am working on: mid-twentieth century, non-figurative geometric art, by a British woman in a European context.[71] Moss was a significant and singular figure – she made art that embodies 'space, movement, light' and participated in the seminal exhibitions of the international Constructivist movement: *Konstruktivisten* in Basel 1937 and *Abstrakte Kunst* at Amsterdam's Stedelijk Museum in 1938. She was a founder member of the Paris association *Abstraction-Création*, and the London branch of *Groupe Espace*. Calling her 'the female British Mondrian' reflects the way writing about Moss has almost always sought to define her in relation to him. 'Even feminist art historians must begin with the developing tradition of masculine Western art, and so must argue from the men back towards the women. As the men are so much better known, the character of their work is more deeply stamped upon our consciousness and it is hard to discern what is genuinely original in retrospect.'[72]

Moss has, however, retained a presence; works by her have appeared consistently in international exhibitions since the 1960s, at least once or twice a decade, and now more frequently.[73] There have been significant solo shows at the Zürich Museum Haus Konstruktiv (2017) and Tate St Ives in the UK (touring to Leeds Art Gallery, Jerwood Hastings and Tate Britain 2013–15) (Figs 31–2). She was represented many times over in the celebrations to mark the centenary of *De Stijl*: Moss works, from their respective collections, were on the wall at the Stedelijk in Amsterdam and the Gemeentemuseum in The Hague, alongside the more famous names, and she was included in *Iconoplastic: 100 Years of De Stijl*, at Sotheby's in New York, in 2017. Moss also featured in the UK-touring Tate St Ives show *Virginia Woolf: An Exhibition Inspired by her Writings*, as well as the Tate Britain exhibition *Queer British Art* – a feminist context and a queer one respectively.[74] With the resurgence of feminism in the era of #MeToo and concurrent trans questioning of the

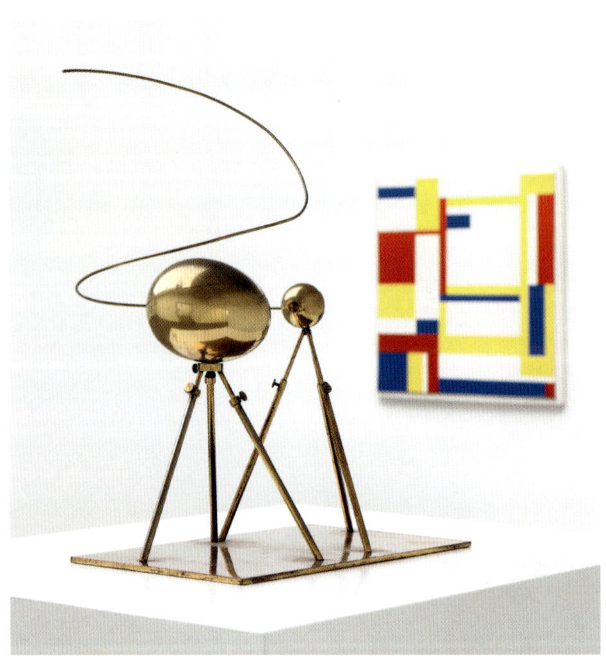

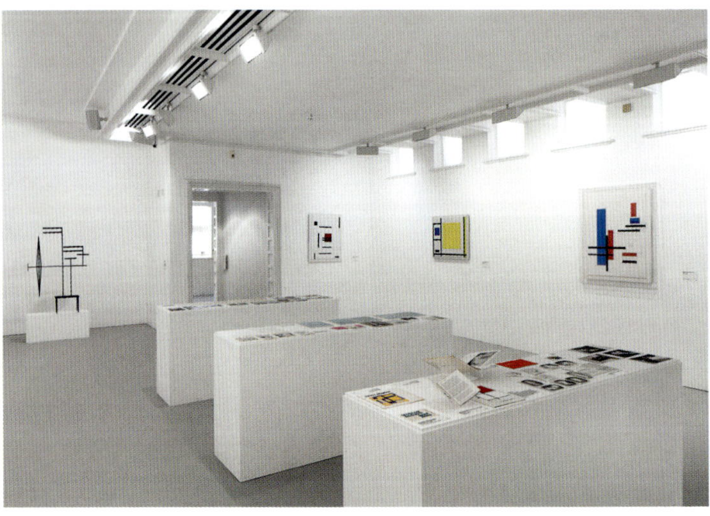

appropriateness of gendered pronouns,[75] her inclusion in exhibitions and indeed the first run of this series of books 'Modern Women Artists', cements this renewal of interest in Moss's life and work. Depending on the fashions of the art world, and the market, Moss's oeuvre will be increasingly rediscovered, and reinterpreted. The discrete contributions she made to Constructivism in the 1930s are finally defined, particularly the double-line; but her lasting legacy is as yet undecided.

'Art is as – Life – forever in the state of Becoming.'[76]

31. (above) Exhibition view, Museum Haus Konstruktiv, 2017
32. (below) Exhibition view, Tate St Ives, 2013

Notes

1 Moss quoted from memory by AH Nijhoff in her catalogue essay 'Marlow Moss' (Amsterdam 1962).

2 An exploration of another of these portraits can be found in Sarah Wilson's essay 'Feminities – Masquerades', Jennifer Blessing (ed.), *Rrose Is a Rrose Is a Rrose: Gender Performance in Photography* (New York 1997), p.137.

3 Moss quoted from memory, Nijhoff (cited note 1).

4 See Ankie de Jongh-Vermeulen, 'Miss Marlow Moss En Mondriaan', *Vrij Nederland*, 7 Jan 1994, pp.48–51; and Florette Dijkstra, *The Sequel* (trans. Penny Maddrell) ('s-Hertogenbosch 1997), p.32.

5 It has been argued that the mythologising-of-self is a tactical strategy engaged by lesbian artists to establish a distinct lesbian genealogy, because 'mythology is history'. See Charlotte Wolff, *Love Between Women* (New York 1971), cited in Tirza True Latimer, *Women Together/Women Apart: Portraits of Lesbian Paris* (New Brunswick, New Jersey and London 2005), pp.9, 37.

6 John Russell, 'Predicaments', *The Sunday Times*, 22 Nov 1953.

7 An example being: GS Whittet, 'London Commentary', *Studio*, vol. 147, Feb 1954; Cablegram, August 1942, in the Alfred H. Barr, Jr. Papers: AAA AHB 2168; Frames 32 and 33, the Museum of Modern Art Archives, New York.

8 Virginia Woolf's character Orlando is an appropriate comparison, as is the Czech artist Toyen, who took her name from the French word *citoyen*, which offered a non-gendered identity.

9 This is a letter to Georges Vantongerloo (2 Oct 1934), Vantongerloo Collection, Haus Bill, Zumikon.

10 Descendants have referred to Moss as 'Aunt Marjorie' in correspondence with the author.

11 Tate Archives, London.

12 Marlow Moss, Issue 1, *abstraction-création: art non-figuratif* (Paris 1932).

13 Moss quoted from memory, Nijhoff (cited note 1).

14 Ibid.

15 Letter dated 1933, in Marianne Le Pommeré, *L'oeuvre de Jean Gorin* (Zürich 1985), L.28, pp.497–8.

16 Letter dated 31 Jan [?] 1934, ibid., L.31, p.499.

17 Letter dated 8 Jun 1935, from Mondrian to Ella and Louise Hoyack, *De Stijl* Archives of the Rijksbureau voor Kunsthistorische Documentatie, The Hague.
18 Mondrian, in a letter to Louis and Ella Hoyack, undated (c.Oct 1931), copy in the RKD, The Hague.
19 Two letters (15 May 1941 and 24 Sep 1941), private collection.
20 Nijhoff (cited note 1).
21 Letter from Vantongerloo to Gorin (16 Apr 1937), Le Pommeré (cited note 15), L.62D, p.514.
22 Letter from Mondrian to Gorin (18 Nov 1936), ibid., L36, p.501.
23 Vantongerloo to Gorin (cited note 21).
24 Gabo quoted in Tom Cross, *Painting the Warmth of the Sun: St. Ives Artists 1939–1979* (Penzance/Guildford 1984), p.53.
25 Nijhoff (cited note 1).
26 Cor Blok, *Piet Mondriaan: Een catalogus van zijn werk in Nederlands openbaar bezit* (Amsterdam 1974), p.68.
27 Christopher Green, 'Léger and L'Esprit Nouveau', John Golding and Christopher Green, *Léger and Purist Paris* (London 1970), p.70.
28 Nijhoff (cited note 1).
29 Charles Harrison, 'Mondrian in London', *Studio International*, vol. 172, no. 884, 1966, p.285, amongst many examples.
30 Robert P. Welsh, 'The Place of Composition 12 with Small Blue Square in the Art of Piet Mondrian', *National Gallery of Canada Bulletin and Annual Bulletin*, no. 29, 1977, pp.3–32.
31 Yves-Alain Bois, 'The Iconoclast', Yves-Alain Bois et al., *Piet Mondrian 1872–1944* (Boston, New York, Toronto, London 1994), fn 156, p.371; and Chronology, p.62.
32 Carel Blotkamp, *Mondrian: The Art of Destruction* (trans. Barbara Potter Fasting) (London 1994), p.201.
33 Ibid., p.218.
34 Ibid., p.229.
35 The earliest example being Kati Rötger, 'Nachwort-Anmerkungen zum Titelbild: *White, Black, Red and Grey* von Marlow Moss', in Rötger and Heike Paul (eds), *Differenzen in der Geschlechterdifferenz – Aktuelle Perspektiven der Geschlechterforschung* (Berlin 1999). The theme has now been revisited, and examined in a wider context of contemporary gender discourse, by Jessica Schouela, 'Marlow Moss: Transgender and the Double Line', *Women's Art Journal*, Fall/Winter 2018, vol. 39, issue 2, pp.34–42.
36 The 1957 painting *Black, Yellow, Blue and White* is the only work to represent Moss in Herbert Read, *A Concise History of Modern Painting*, 1959/1968 (London 1974), p.357. Read does not mention Moss in other publications (*Modern Sculpture: a Concise History*, and his *Dictionary of Art and Artists*).
37 Mondrian supplied Moss with the address of Mr and Mrs Nicholson in a letter dated 15 May 1941, private collection.

38 Three letters from Moss to Nicholson, from 1941, 1942 and 1943, are held in
    the Tate Archives, London.
39 John Lesley Martin, Ben Nicholson and Naum Gabo (eds), *Circle:
    International Survey of Constructive Art* (London 1937).
40 These episodes are recorded in Florette Dijkstra, Marlow Moss: *Constructivist
    + the Reconstruction Project* (trans. Annie Wright) ('s-Hertogenbosch
    1995), p.22. Dijkstra's account stems particularly from a letter from the
    artist Michael Canney, curator of the Newlyn Art Gallery from 1956–64,
    that she received in the mid-1990s stating 'somebody told me that
    Nicholson did try to interest [Moss] in showing in St Ives, without success'.
    In an earlier letter from Canney to 'Robert' (14 Nov 1990), Canney states
    the same (a copy of this letter is held in the Women's Art Library,
    Goldsmiths). The claim is repeated in another letter from Canney to the
    artist Tam Giles (16 May 1994), and is reiterated in a letter to a 'Miss Shaw'
    (6 Nov 1995, Women's Art Library), adding that Moss 'avoided all societies'.
    I think, by this point, what started as a vague memory had solidified
    through the re-telling of the story; Moss did not avoid all societies,
    she was a member of several in her lifetime; it may be true, however,
    that she avoided the Penwith Society.
41 Canney mentions this in the letter to Miss Shaw cited above; he does not
    say when Nicholson said this to him, or explain what he thought Nicholson
    meant by it.
42 Letter from Moss to Vantongerloo, undated [1944?], Vantongerloo Archive,
    Haus Bill, Zumikon.
43 'They [Moss and Stanley Gardiner] always remained friends and she would
    come to our house and we would go to hers for meals etc.', Keith Gardiner,
    A Painter's Paradise: Memories of an Artist's Son Growing up in Lamorna
    (2005).
44 Information gleaned from speaking with Lamorna residents.
45 Moss mentions Colquhoun in letters to Paule Vézelay held in the Tate
    Archives (2 Nov 1954; 3 Jul 1955; 19 Aug 1955; 11 Mar 1957). A letter from Moss
    to Gabo (19 Apr 1945) is held in the Beinecke Rare Book and Manuscript
    Library, Yale University (microfiche copy, Tate Archives).
46 Letter from Moss to Vantongerloo, undated [1944?], Vantongerloo Archive,
    Haus Bill, Zumikon.
47 The Duchesse de la Salle is perhaps best known now from her 1925 portrait
    by Tamara de Lempicka.
48 Ithell Colquhoun, 'The Streams of St Bride', unpublished manuscript, Tate
    Archives.
49 See Dijkstra (cited note 4).
50 Marlow Moss, exhibition of drawings and constructions, 17 Feb–17 Mar 1949,
    Mousehole: Arra Gallery, Tate Archives.

51 Jean-Yves Mock, who included Moss in an article for *Apollo*, was Brausen's assistant; 'La Peinture Abstraite Géométrique', *Apollo*, vol. 68, Dec 1958, pp.215–16.

52 This information was gleaned from the Hanover Gallery Collection of the Tate Archives. Brausen's gallery merged with Gimpel Fils in the early 1970s, and was for a time active in Zürich as the Gimpel & Hanover Galerie, run by Anne Rotzler, where Moss's work was given a solo show in 1973.

53 As described by Jean-Yves Mock in a letter to the author (13 Apr 2008).

54 See Alan Fowler, 'A Forgotten British Constructivist Group: The London Branch of Groupe Espace, 1953–59', *The Burlington Magazine*, vol. CXLIX, no. 1248, Mar 2007.

55 This was told to the author by Andreas Oosthoek (having been told to him by Nijhoff herself) during a conversation in Middelburg, Jul 2007.

56 See Judith Butler, *Gender Trouble: Feminism and the Subversion of Identity* (New York and London 1990). The anecdote regarding Moss and Nijhoff's arrest is recounted by Martinus Nijhoff in a letter reproduced in the collection edited by Andreas Oosthoek, *Brieven Aan Mijn Vrouw* (Amsterdam 1996).

57 See Anna C. Chave, 'Minimalism and the Rhetoric of Power', Francis Frascina and Jonathan Harris (eds), *Art in Modern Culture: an Anthology of Critical Texts* (London 1992), p.270. In a later essay, 'Minimalism and Biography', *The Art Bulletin*, vol. LXXXII, issue 1, 2000, pp.149–63, Chave argues that she did not 'caricature or categorically condemn Minimalism as a 'macho' enterprise', fn 57, p.162. She does however seem to assume its masculine nature.

58 Germaine Greer, *The Obstacle Race* (London 1979), p.103.

59 The *Marlow Moss Reconstructieproject*, by Florette Dijkstra, was exhibited at the Gemeentemuseum in Arnhem 1994–5, and then at Tate St Ives in 1998.

60 The operetta *De schrijver, zijn vrouw, haar minnares*, by Anna Maria Versloot and Douwe Eisenga, was performed at the Zeeland Nazomerfestival in Aug/Sep 2014; *Living Ingredient* was performed by the Pure Dance Company at the opening of the exhibition in Arnhem, 1994. Primitive World, *White On White*, LP, Ecstatic Recordings, was released in 2018.

61 Paintings by Sudaporn Teja in tribute to Moss were shown at *LGBTQ: Loves Get Better with Time Quietly*, Serindia Gallery, Bangkok, 2018. The exhibition *Conversations Around Marlow Moss*, curated by artists Katrina Blannin and Andrew Bick at & Model Gallery in Leeds, coincided with the Leeds Art Gallery show *Parallel Lives: Marlow Moss & Claude Cahun*, 6 Jun– 7 Sep 2014, and featured the installation by Cullinan Richards *Savage School Lightbox: MARLOW MOSS 2014*. Other examples are the exhibitions *Larry Bell and Sarah Crowner, Meet Marlow Moss* (Kunstverein, Amsterdam, 18 May–22 Jun 2013) and *O-MUSE!* (Frans Hals Museum, Haarlem, 6 Jun–

30 Aug 2015). Moss also features in a zine produced by Camden Arts Centre for Amy Sillman: *Landline* (Sep 2018–Jan 2019).

62 Tom Lubbock, 'The Project: To Reconstruct Lost Works of a Dead and Unjustly Neglected Artist. The Result: A Case of Misattribution or Just Mistaken Identity?', *The Independent*, 9 Dec 1997, Features, p.14.

63 Rex Butler, 'Unerasure', Brad Buckley and John Conomos (eds), *Erasure: the Spectre of Cultural Memory* (Faringdon 2015), pp.152–3.

64 Donald K. McNamee uses Moss as an example this way, in his argument against the primacy of the written 'document' in art history, in a review of Stephen Bann's survey, 'The Tradition of Constructivism', *The Structurist*, no. 15/16 (double issue), 1975/1976, pp.167–73. Moss is again used as an example, but this time to confront the formation of histories in general, in Greer (cited note 58), p.103.

65 Mondrian advised Moss on how to obtain papers from the American Consulate, and then an exit permit from the English Consulate, in a letter dated 15 May 1941, private collection.

66 Vantongerloo proposed a joint exhibition of himself and Moss in a letter to Pierre Matisse, New York, dated 17 Jun 1938, Vantongerloo Archive, Haus Bill, Zumikon.

67 Although her name does appear momentarily at the back of the book in a list of artists taking part in the exhibition *Konstruktivisten* at the Kunsthalle in Basel (cited note 39).

68 Jane Beckett in her essay 'Circle: The Theory and Patronage of Constructive Art in the Thirties' acknowledges that Moss 'might reasonably have been included', in *Circle: Constructive Art in Britain 1934–40*, Jeremy Lewison (ed.), (Cambridge 1982), p.18.

69 Charles Biederman, *Art as the Evolution of Visual Knowledge* (Minnesota 1948); George Rickey, *Constructivism: Origins and Evolution* (New York 1995); Anthony Hill (ed.), *Data: Directions in Art, Theory and Aesthetics: An Anthology* (London 1968).

70 Stephen Bann (ed.), *The Tradition of Constructivism* (London 1974).

71 This is in reference to the essay by Mary D. Sherif, '*"So What Are You Working On"*: Categorizing the Exceptional Woman', Kristen Frederickson and Sarah E. Webb (eds), *Singular Women: Writing the Artist* (Berkeley, Los Angeles and London 2003), pp.48–65.

72 Greer (cited note 58), p.103. Greer, who championed Moss so effectively as a feminist, is now maligned by sections of the trans community having been 'no-platformed' as a 'terf' at Cardiff University in 2015; this episode is emblematic of the fractures that Moss straddles.

73 Some examples: AM Hammacher, *Mondrian, De Stijl and Their Impact* (New York 1964); Norbert Nobis and Gladys C. Fabre, *Abstraction Création: 1931–1936* (Paris/Münster 1978); Gladys C. Fabre (ed.), *Paris: Arte Abstracto – Arte Concreto – Cercle Et Carré – 1930* (Valencia 1990). Moss is included in the

exhibition catalogue: Gladys Fabre and Doris Wintgens Hötte (eds),
*Theo van Doesburg and the International Avant-Garde: Constructing a
New World* (London 2009), but not illustrated; she is mentioned in the text
(p.18), and also in the Artist Biographies section (p.236). There is an entry
for Moss written by Margreeth Soeting, in RH Fuchs et al., *Als Golfslag Op
Het Strand ... (Waves Breaking on the Shore) Ad Dekkers in Zijn Tijd,*
(trans. Anthony Fudge, Ruth Koenig and Yvonne van Limburg) (Amsterdam
1998), pp.156–7.

74 Laura Smith, Enrico Tassi and Eloise Bennett (eds), *Virginia Woolf* exhibition
catalogue (London 2018); Clare Barlow (ed.), *Queer British Art 1861–1967*
(London 2017); Alex Pilcher, *A Queer Little History of Art* (London 2017).

75 The Henry Moore Institute Collection in Leeds was prompted to change a
wall label for their Moss sculpture on display, in 2018, in order to avoid the
use of pronouns; in an accompanying statement it was acknowledged
that Moss, in name and title, chose not to be categorised according to
gender, and that there is wider debate still to be had.

76 Marlow Moss, *Abstract Art*, unpublished manuscript, *c.*1955,
private collection.

Image credits

1. Stephen Storm, *Portrait photograph of Marlow Moss (leaning on her hand)*, c.1938, private collection.
2. *abstraction-création: art non-figuratif*, Issue 1, 1932, Paris, p.26 (showing two paintings, both dated 1931), published source.
3. *White, Black, Red and Grey*, 1932, oil on canvas, 44.5 × 54 cm, Gemeentemuseum Collection, The Hague, The Netherlands.
4. *Composition With Blue Surface*, 1934, oil on canvas, 45 × 62 cm, Museum van Hedendaagse Kunst Antwerpen (MuHKA), Antwerp (Stadhuis Middelburg Collection), Collection Vleeshal, Middelburg, The Netherlands. Given as permanent loan to MuHKA Museum of Contemporary Art, Antwerp.
5. *White, Red and Black*, 1942, oil on canvas with wooden strips, 76 × 76 cm, The Israel Museum, Jerusalem. B72.1164. Photo © The Israel Museum, Jerusalem by Elie Posner.
6. *White, Black, Yellow and Blue*, 1954, oil on canvas, 46 × 61 cm, private collection, UK. Image courtesy of Offer Waterman & Co.
7. *Composition in Blue, Black, Yellow, Red and White*, 1956–7, oil on canvas, 92 × 68.5 cm, The Israel Museum, Jerusalem. B72.1165. Photo © The Israel Museum, Jerusalem by Elie Posner.
8. *Red, Blue, Yellow and White*, 1957–8, oil on canvas, 91.5 × 68.5 cm, Collection Stedelijk Museum Amsterdam.
9. *Linear Construction*, 1956–7, steel, with aluminium bases, 65.1 × 37.2 × 23.2 cm, The Kröller-Müller Museum, Otterlo (Donated by Ida and Piet Sanders in 1987). KM 115.802.
10. *[Triangles on Points]*, 1942–3, painted metal, dimensions unknown, private collection.
11. *[Triangles on edges]*, 1942–3, painted metal, dimensions unknown, private collection.
12. Marlow Moss's studio in Lamorna, c.1956–8, private collection.
13. Marlow Moss's studio in Lamorna, c.1956–8, private collection.
14. *White with Curved Cord*, c.1936, oil on canvas with cord, 103.5 × 73 cm, The Kröller-Müller Museum, Otterlo (Donated by Ida and Piet Sanders in 1987). KM 103.268.

15. *White with Rope*, 1940, oil on canvas with rope, 54 × 54 cm, The Riklis Collection of McCrory Corporation. Acc. no.: 1053.1983. New York, Museum of Modern Art (MoMA). © 2019. Digital image, The Museum of Modern Art, New York/Scala, Florence.
16. *Composition in Yellow, Black and White*, 1949, oil paint and wood on canvas, 50.8 × 35.6 × 0.6 cm © Tate, London 2019.
17. Marika de la Salle, Netty Nijhoff, Ireen Farjon and Marlow Moss, c.1950s, private collection.
18. *Sculptural Form*, 1943, white marble © Tate, London 2019.
19. *[Untitled]*, 1942, ink and gouache on paper, 34.4 × 49.7 cm, Ville de Grenoble/Musée de Grenoble–J.L. Lacroix.
20. *Zeichnung Nr 3*, 1943, ink and gouache on paper, 34.6 × 50 cm, Ville de Grenoble/Musée de Grenoble–J.L. Lacroix.
21. *Work on Paper, no. 3, Untitled*, 1943, pencil, crayon and gouache on paper, courtesy of The Mayor Gallery, London.
22. *Untitled*, 1946, pencil and crayon on paper, private collection, UK.
23. *Balanced Forms in Gunmetal on Cornish Granite*, 1956–7, metal and granite, 22 × 33 × 28.5 cm © Tate, London 2019.
24. *Free Relief*, 1957, painted wood and aluminium, 51 × 108 x 12.5 cm, The Kröller-Müller Museum, Otterlo (purchased from AH Nijhoff, 1965). KM 112.222.
25. *Spatial Construction in Steel*, 1956–8, steel, 80 x 128 cm, Leeds Museums and Galleries (Leeds Art Gallery) UK / Leeds Museums and Galleries, UK / Bridgeman Images.
26. *No.31 preliminary drawing for oil*, c.1954, pencil and gouache on paper, private collection, London. Courtesy of The Mayor Gallery.
27. *No.34 preliminary drawing for oil*, c.1956, pencil, collage and gouache on paper, private collection, London. Courtesy of The Mayor Gallery.
28. *Untitled*, c.1950s, brass on wooden base, 21.4 × 9.3 × 8.8 cm, Tate, purchased with funds provided by the Denise Coates Foundation on the occasion of the 2018 centenary of women gaining the right to vote in Britain.
29. Florette Dijkstra, *The Marlow Moss Reconstructionproject*, 1994. Photograph taken by the artist, at her home, Den Bosch, NL.
30. Andrew Bick, *For Marlow Moss*, 2018, aluminium, bronze, glass and stainless steel, Princes Arcade, Piccadilly, London. Commissioned by the Crown Estate, in collaboration with Rolfe Judd Architects, curated by Modus Operandi. Image courtesy of the artist.
31. Exhibition view, Museum Haus Konstruktiv, showing Moss sculpture and painting, 2017. Photo © Stefan Altenburger. *Construction Spatial*, 1953, brass, private collection, UK, and *Composition in Red, Yellow, Blue and White*, 1956–7, oil on canvas, The Israel Museum, Jerusalem, gift of WS Nijhoff, Biggekerke, NL, through Dr Willem Sandberg, Amsterdam.
32. Tate St Ives Summer exhibition, 2013. Installation view of Marlow Moss artwork, Room 1, 2013. Photograph © Tate, London 2019.

About the author

Lucy Howarth completed her PhD thesis on Marlow Moss in 2008, and, after a period in the Tate Research Department, co-curated the Moss display, which toured from Tate St Ives, to Leeds Art Gallery, the Jerwood Gallery in Hastings and Tate Britain 2013–15. Lucy was consultant curator for the 2017 Moss exhibition at Museum Haus Konstruktiv, Zürich. She has taught in Fine Art and Art History departments at various universities, and currently runs a contemporary art project space in Margate.

Acknowledgements

Many thanks to Florette Dijkstra, whose work was the starting point for my research on Moss. Thanks to all the artists, curators, academics, archivists, librarians, conservators, writers and collectors I have met along the way, amongst them: Sam Smiles, Laura Smith, Ankie de Jongh-Vermeulen, Andreas Oosthoek, Jean-Yves Mock, Mike Weston, Sabine Schaschl, Tim Bent, Sacha Llewellyn, Andrew Bick, Flip Feij, Matthijs Erdman, Chris Stephens and Chris Green.

The collections we have referred to, including: Gemeentemuseum, The Hague; Museum van Hedendaagse Kunst, Antwerp; Stadhuis Middelburg; Kröller-Müller Museum, Otterlo; Museum of Modern Art, New York; Israel Museum, Jerusalem; Tate, London; Stedelijk Museum, Amsterdam; Mayor Gallery, London; Leeds Museums and Galleries; Musée de Grenoble, France; Museum Haus Konstruktiv, Zürich.

Particular mention to Adrian Glew and Tate Archives; Wietse Coppes (Rijksbureau voor Kunsthistorische Documentatie, The Hague) and Leo Jansen (Huygens Institute for the History of the Netherlands), editors of the Mondrian Edition Project, for the transcripts of letters pertaining to Moss; Richard Shillitoe who drew my attention to unpublished Ithell Colquhoun manuscripts; and also Althea Greenan and the Women's Art Library, Goldsmiths, University of London – a remarkable resource for the history of art made by women.

Special thanks to Hazel Rank-Broadley and her family.

Index

Marlow Moss
by Lucy Howarth
First Edition

First published in the United Kingdom in 2019 by Eiderdown Books
eiderdownbooks.com

Series conceived and developed by Eiderdown Books
Text copyright © Lucy Howarth and Eiderdown Books, 2019
Images copyright © the estate of the artist

The moral right of the author has been asserted

All rights reserved. No part of this publication may be reproduced,
stored in a retrieval system, or transmitted in any form or by any means,
electronic, mechanical, photocopying, recording or otherwise, without the
prior written permission from the publisher and copyright owners.

Every effort has been made to ensure images are correctly
attributed however if any omission or error has been made please
notify the publisher for correction in future editions.

A CIP catalogue record for this book is available from the British Library

ISBN: 978-1-9160416-2-2

Series Editor: Katy Norris
Editor: Rebeka Cohen
Indexder: Hilary Bird
Series design by Clare Skeats
Typeset by Clare Skeats in Lelo by Katharina Köhler

The Modern Women Artists logotype is set in Hesse Antiqua,
which was released in 2018 to mark the 100th birthday of
Gudrun Zapf von Hesse. The forms of Hesse Antiqua are based
on the metal punches that von Hesse created in 1947, while working
as a bookbinder at the Bauer Type Foundry in Frankfurt.

Printed and bound by Imago
Reprographics by ALTA